Philosophy and
the Young Child

Philosophy and the Young Child

Gareth B. Matthews

HARVARD UNIVERSITY PRESS
Cambridge, Massachusetts
and London, England
1980

Copyright © 1980 by the President
and Fellows of Harvard College
All rights reserved
Printed in the United States of America

Library of Congress Cataloging in Publication Data

Matthews, Gareth B   1929–
  Philosophy and the young child.

  Includes bibliographical references and index.
  1. Children and philosophy. I. Title.
B105.C45M37   108'.8054   80-11494
ISBN 0-674-66605-4

For Mary

Preface

I FIRST BECAME INTERESTED in the philosophical thought of young children by worrying about how to teach introductory courses in philosophy to college students. Many students seemed to resist the idea that doing philosophy could be natural. In response to their resistance I hit on the strategy of showing them that as children many of them had already done philosophy. It occurred to me that my task as a college philosophy teacher was to reintroduce my students to an activity that they had once enjoyed and found natural, but that they had later been socialized to abandon.

Once I began ruminating on philosophical thinking in children, I found the subject fascinating. I also found that it interested others, both inside and outside the classroom. So I began to develop my ideas about it, to do some informal research and teaching on the subject, and to gather the reactions and thoughts of others—philosophers and nonphilosophers, parents, teachers, and simply people who like children.

In writing this little book I have been encouraged by the interest of many people, especially Paul Bosley, Stanley Cavell, Herbert Kohl, Matthew Lipman, Mary Matthews, and William Winslade. For supplying me with some of the anecdotes I wish to thank Stephen Brown, John Cooper,

Mary Fairfield, Eileen Kologinsky, Jane and Michael Martin, Andy Martinez, and John Robison.

Parts of this book first appeared in the following publications: *Communication and Understanding,* edited by Godfrey Vesey (Sussex: Harvester Press, 1977); the journal *Metaphilosophy,* volumes 7 (1976) and 10 (1979); the journal *Thinking,* volume 1 (1979); and *Growing Up with Philosophy,* edited by Matthew Lipman and Ann Margaret Sharp (Philadelphia: Temple University Press, 1978). I wish to thank the director of the Royal Institute of Philosophy, the editor of *Metaphysics,* the editor of *Thinking,* and Temple University Press for permission to use these materials here. I also wish to thank Routledge & Kegan Paul Ltd and Basic Books, Inc., for permission to quote passages and to reprint an illustration from *The Child's Conception of the World* by Jean Piaget; and Routledge & Kegan Paul Ltd and Schocken Books, Inc., for permission to quote from *Intellectual Growth in Young Children* by Susan Isaacs.

Amherst, Massachusetts   G.B.M.
May 1980

Contents

Philosophy and the Young Child

1. Puzzlement

TIM (about six years), while busily engaged in licking a pot, asked, "Papa, how can we be sure that everything is not a dream?"

NO DOUBT it seems to Tim that he is busily engaged in licking a pot. If he were dreaming, he would, presumably, be dreaming that he is busily engaged in licking a pot. What is the difference between really licking a pot and only dreaming that one is doing so? Perhaps the difference is only this: if one is dreaming, one may wake up from the dream and then know that the pot-licking episode was only a dream.

Does it, or should it, make any difference to Tim to know whether he is awake or dreaming? If so, what difference? Wouldn't the pot taste just as good?[1]

I have been talking as though Tim's question were "How do I know whether I am now dreaming?" But, of course, it isn't that. Rather, it is this: "How can we be sure that not *everything* is a dream?" That is, how can we be sure that we are ever awake?

Suppose that everything is a dream, my dream. There would be parts of my dream in which I seem to be awake and parts of it in which I seem to be asleep. What could be the difference between life as I now believe it to be, with its waking periods and its dream episodes, and a lifelong dream in which I seem sometimes to be awake and sometimes to have dreamt this or that?

Tim's puzzle is quintessentially philosophical. Tim has framed a question that calls into doubt a very ordinary notion (being awake) in such a way as to make us wonder whether we really know something that most of us unquestioningly assume we know. What it makes us wonder is whether we know that we are sometimes awake and that, therefore, not all life is a dream.

Puzzlement and wonder are closely related. Aristotle says that philosophy begins in wonder (*Metaphysics* 982b12). Bertrand Russell tells us that philosophy, "if it cannot *answer* so many questions as we could wish, has at least the power of *asking* questions which increase the interest of the world, and show the strangeness and wonder lying just below the surface even in the commonest things of daily life."[2]

Aristotle also suggests that the wonder that initiates philosophy is akin to puzzlement (*Metaphysics* 982b17–18). And Wittgenstein says, "A philosophical problem has the form: 'I don't know my way about.' "[3]

Sometimes philosophical puzzlement is dissolved. One learns to find one's way about; perhaps one reasons one's way out of the difficulty. But sometimes the puzzlement is not dissolved, at least not for a long time.

> JORDAN (five years), going to bed at eight one evening, asked, "If I go to bed at eight and get up at seven in the morning, how do I really know that the little hand of the clock has gone around only once? Do I have to stay up all night to watch it? If I look away even for a short time, maybe the small hand will go around twice."

In part, perhaps, Jordan's puzzlement rests on an unease about not having enough evidence, or maybe not enough evidence of the right sort, to draw a commonsense conclusion, namely, the conclusion that between a given night and the next morning the little hand of the clock goes around once and only once.

Usually, one's observations of a clock are sporadic. Jordan, for example, may check on his clock from time to time during the day, but not, obviously, when he is out of the room: not when he eats his meals, watches television, goes out to play or off to school. In principle Jordan could surely devote a whole day to watching his clock. He could ask that his meals be brought to his bedroom, or he could take his clock with him to the dinner table. By these means Jordan could keep the clock under constant surveillance.

Jordan's final comment—"If I look away even for a short time, maybe the small hand will go around twice"— suggests that his problem may not be the practical one of, as a philosopher of science might say, enlarging his evidence base. Rather, it suggests that no matter how much constant attention Jordan lavishes on his clock, there may still be a worry about how he can justifiably extrapolate from observed periods to unobserved ones.

Are observed states and actions a reliable guide to unobserved states and actions? Jordan may have a friend at kindergarten who manages to make faces at the teacher whenever her back is turned, and not otherwise. How do we know that clocks are not like that? *Do* we know that they aren't? Maybe induction rests on an assumption as naive as the belief that what Jordan and his friend do under the watchful eye of the teacher is a reliable guide to what they do when the teacher leaves the room or looks away.

I don't know whether Jordan found a way to deal with

his puzzlement. Perhaps he did, or perhaps he eventually lost interest in it. If, someday, he takes a college philosophy course, he may find that it includes discussion of what is called "the problem of induction." Stripped to its essentials, this is a problem of saying whether, and if so, on what basis, we can be justified in taking observed instances as a guide to unobserved instances. Jordan may find in the problem of induction an old friend. Of course, by the time Jordan gets to college, he may have forgotten that he had ever worried about the unobserved behavior of his clock.

> ONE DAY John Edgar (four years), who had often seen airplanes take off, rise, and gradually disappear into the distance, took his first plane ride. When the plane stopped ascending and the seat-belt sign went out, John Edgar turned to his father and said in a rather relieved, but still puzzled, tone of voice, "Things don't really get smaller up here."

Philosophers and psychologists have long debated whether an airplane disappearing into the distance seems to be getting smaller and we learn to interpret the appearance of a shrinking object as a case of an object receding into space, or whether, after we have had sufficient experience with objects moving away from us and coming toward us, the airplane simply seems to be receding into the distance and no inference or interpretation is required.

The first idea fits a philosophical reconstruction of our knowledge according to whether we receive data through our senses that are in themselves incorrigible (that is, we know infallibly how things *seem* to us) and we make inferences from these data to the reality that lies behind them (in this case, to the conclusion that the airplane is really going farther and farther away from us). According to this view, the mistakes we make about the world we perceive around us arise from the inferences we draw from incorrigible and indubitable data.

Opponents of this sense-datum view insist that it is impossible to isolate the pure datum of sense experience and distinguish it from all interpretations we put on it and from all inferences we draw from it. According to them, once we have had experience with receding objects, the objects do not appear to shrink when they recede; they simply appear to recede.

The disagreement between the two sides is important in epistemology, the theory of knowledge. The sense-datum view is obviously friendly to the idea that we could reconstruct all our knowledge of the world around us in such a way as to show that it rests on secure foundations, sense data. The other view considers foundationalism in epistemology naive and misconceived.

John Edgar's comment suggests that a much more nearly pure "given" is available to him than the critics of the sense-datum theory suppose is available. Moreover, his comment indicates that he may have put a wrong interpretation on his data and is in the process of working out another interpretation.

Do airplanes really shrink as they go up into the sky? If they did, how would they look, up in the sky, to the passengers they are carrying? Surely the passengers too would shrink. Looking at themselves and at the inside of the plane, they might be in no better position to detect the shrinkage than Alice was in Wonderland:

> Soon her eye fell on a little glass box that was lying under the table: she opened it, and found in it a very small cake, on which the words "EAT ME" were beautifully marked in currants. "Well, I'll eat it," said Alice,

"and if it makes me grow larger, I can reach the key; and if it makes me grow smaller, I can creep under the door; so either way I'll get into the garden, and I don't care which happens!"

She ate a little bit, and said anxiously to herself "Which way? Which way?" holding her hand on the top of her head to feel which way it was growing, and she was quite surprised to find that she remained the same size.[4]

If John Edgar's conclusion is based simply on how things look in the cabin around him, his inference is just as shaky as Alice's. No doubt, however, he will soon have a look out the window. Perhaps he will see the airport from which the plane took off. He will see that the people and the planes still on the ground have "shrunk" in much the way that airplanes "shrink" into the distance when he himself is on the ground. Reflection on these data may lead him to distinguish appearance from reality and to infer that receding objects seem to get smaller even though they actually maintain their size.

WHEN I TAUGHT "Philosophy and the Young Child" at Smith College several years ago, one of my students decided to try out some of the questions we were discussing on her five-year-old brother, David. During spring vacation she interviewed him and recorded the exchange. In the transcript is an instructive moment of puzzlement over the concept of life:

DAVID worries about whether an apple is alive. He decides that it is when it's on the ground but not when it has been brought into the house.

Is the apple on the table alive? David is puzzled. If it is alive, then when we eat it, we eat something that is alive. If it isn't, how does it differ from an apple still hanging from a tree?

A common approach to the question of life is to list several "life" functions (digestion, elimination, reproduction, locomotion) and then say that an organism is alive if it is capable of performing several of those functions. David seems not to have had that kind of approach in mind. What did he have in mind?

Consider flowers. When we cut roses, bring them inside, and put them in water in a vase, we say that we are keeping them alive (at least until the petals begin to fall and the leaves to turn brown).

We don't put apples in water. We might put them in a cool place, but we don't say that we are doing this to keep them alive—only, perhaps, to keep them fresh. Do they, then, cease to be alive when we bring them indoors?

Are apples alive when they lie on the ground? Perhaps David thinks of an apple's being alive in terms of its life cycle. He may know that the apple contains seeds and nourishment for the seeds and that, if an apple is left on the ground, a seed may eventually germinate and produce a little apple tree. This little tree may grow into a big one and, in turn, produce apples of its own. In this way the cycle goes on.

Perhaps one could say that death occurs when the cycle is interrupted, for example, when the sapling withers so that it will not grow into a tree or when the apple is brought indoors so that its seeds will not germinate. This suggestion is an interesting one, an ingenious response to a very old and very persistent puzzle.

I AM TUCKING my eight-year-old son, John, in bed. He looks up at me and asks, quite without warning, "Daddy, why don't I see you double, because I have two eyes and I can see you with each one by itself?"

What do I say?

First, I try to make sure that I understand what is puzzling him.

"You have two ears," I point out. "Are you surprised you don't *hear* double?"

John grins. "What is hearing double?"

"Well, maybe my-my voi-voice wo-would s-sound li-like thi-this," I say.

He reflects. "But your ears both go to the same place."

"And couldn't it be that your eyes both go to the same place?" I suggest.

He gets serious, thinks, then grins again. "You're just giving me another problem," he protests. "I want to think about the one I already have."

Fair enough. "Maybe," I suggest, "it's because the picture you get with your left eye comes together with the picture you get with your right eye. When they come together they make *one* picture."

We experiment with two fingers, one closer to our eyes, the other farther away. We try focusing now on one, now on the other. The aim is to see how, by focusing on the nearer finger, we can see the farther one double and vice versa. The moral is supposed to be that the two pictures don't *always* come together to make one, though they usually do.

My son is not satisfied. It turns out that he has constructed for himself, elaborating in various ways on what he has learned at school about vision and the retinal image, a complex theory of vision according to which one image comes through each eye, is reversed, rereversed, and then projected in front of the subject. No wonder he is worried about why we don't see double!

I suggest several ways of simplifying his theory, but he won't accept simplifications.

"I'll have to think about it some more," he says. "I'll talk to you again after I get it worked out."

John's question—"Why don't I see you double, because I have two eyes?"—mixes optics, neurophysiology, psychology, and philosophy. John, I discovered, had seen on television at school an episode in which a little man climbed into someone's eye to gaze at the retinal image. Ever since the retinal image was actually observed in the early seventeenth century, people have wondered why they don't see things upside down; after all, the retinal images reverse the objects seen. The seldom-spoken assumption is that what is really seen is the retinal image.

John insisted that the television program he had seen in school had not given him his problem, that he had already had the problem before he saw the program. He certainly seemed willing and able to think of the retinal image as being rereversed by a later process in vision. His problem, he said, was to figure out how the images from the two eyes could merge.

Medieval theorists of vision, such as Alhazen and Roger Bacon, supposed that images travel from each eye through the optic nerve to the optic chiasma, where the two nerves cross and where, as Alhazen and Bacon supposed, the two images become one. It was a worry about why we don't see double even though we receive two images, one through each eye, that led to their theory. It is an answer to John's problem.[5]

In his brilliant *Paralipomena ad vitellionem* Johannes Kepler scathingly rejected this medieval account of vision.

He said that it was optically impossible. Light doesn't behave in the way the medieval theory requires, he explained. Kepler took enormous strides in accounting for the optics of vision, but he did so at a price. He renounced all ambition to give an account of whatever it is that happens after the image is formed on the retina that results in someone's actually seeing something.

John wanted to explain how we see by supposing that we somehow project visual images in front. If we think of images as being projected in this way, somewhat like the image on a movie screen, nothing is explained, for we will want to know how the projected images can be *seen*. Doesn't that require vision, which is just what we first set out to explain? If, however, we think of the frontward projecting as the seeing, then there may be hope for a nonregressive explanation. But the explanation will not be helpful unless we are quite clear about the notion of projection that it uses.

Is John's puzzle a pseudoproblem? Suppose that it is. Then John may one day be sufficiently clear about the optics, neurophysiology, and psychology of vision that he will no longer be puzzled about why we usually don't see double. If that day arrives, he may want to know why he once mistakenly thought that there was a real problem. I hope he will. Trying to say why something one has puzzled over is a mere pseudoproblem is itself often a difficult philosophical task. But it can be rewarding, too.

2. Play

PHILOSOPHY MAY indeed be motivated by puzzlement. But to show that and stop there is to suggest, quite mistakenly, that philosophy is inevitably something terribly serious. In fact, it is often play, conceptual play.

In my course on philosophy and the young child I ask my students to do a certain amount of "lab work." They are to read a story to young children and then, in a very low-pressure way, discuss with the children any philosophical issues the story might suggest. The sister of David, the child who was puzzled about whether the apple was alive, read part of A. A. Milne's *Winnie-the-Pooh* to a group of children six to seven years old at the Smith College Campus School. She conceived the really helpful idea of noting each point in the story at which the children laughed and, afterward, returning to those points and asking the children about the passages.

One passage that caused the children to laugh was the one in which Piglet's grandfather is said to have two names "in case he lost one."[1] My student asked the children if they had two names and if the reason they had more than one were that they might lose one

"No, you can't lose your name," everyone said. Everyone, that is, except Adam.

"What if you forgot it?" asked Adam, suggesting that one way to lose a name might be to forget it.

"Well, then," replied Jennifer, apparently somewhat annoyed at Adam's suggestion, "you could ask your brother."

Adam wasn't satisfied. "But what if *he* forgot it?" Adam persisted mischievously.

"Well, then . . . ," Jennifer's response trailed off into silence.

In her notebook my student commented: "This child's [Adam's] mind has entered the realm of playful possibilities—child philosophy—he seemed to take great *delight* in his questioning."

SUSAN ISAACS'S BOOK *Intellectual Growth in Young Children* contains much evidence of conceptual play. In one passage Denis is ruminating on the relativity of the contrast between being in front and being behind.

> DENIS [four years, six months] was overheard explaining to James that "a thing could be before and behind at the same time". His father asked "How? What do you mean?" . . . They were standing near a table, and Denis said, "Well, supposing we were going round and round the table—now you're in front, and I'm behind—then I'm in front, and you're behind".[2]

Suppose that Denis and James are chasing each other around a table. Suppose that Denis is, so to speak, at three o'clock on the table and James is at nine o'clock and that they are running clockwise. Then, if twelve o'clock is the goal, James is in front and Denis is behind. If, however, six o'clock is the goal, Denis is in front and James is behind. This is the kind of point that Denis's father assumed him to be making: "It was clear from his gestures that, although he could not quite formulate his understanding, he was meaning that 'before' and 'behind' were relative to the point one started reckoning from, on a circle."[3]

Perhaps Denis has something a little different in mind, however. Suppose that Denis and James are chasing each other around a table. And suppose that they are opposite each other and trying to catch each other. Denis, from his point of view, is behind and James is ahead; but James, from his point of view, is behind and Denis is ahead. In other words, Denis, if he is trying to catch James, is behind but is in front if he is trying to escape from James.

Aristotle was the first person to study seriously the logic of relative terms (*Categories,* chap. 7), though puzzles about them certainly played an important role in Plato's thought.[4] Developments in logic during the nineteenth and twentieth centuries have put us in a much better position to understand the puzzles that relative terms engender. But they do nothing to dim the delight that we can have in playfully exploring their perplexities.

EIGHT MONTHS earlier Denis was reflecting on other matters of great logical and metaphysical interest:

> AT TEA, Denis [three years, ten months] said, "The bread's buttered already, isn't it? so if we want it without butter we can't, can we?—unless we 'crape it off wiv a knife . . . and if we want it without butter and don't want to 'crape it off wiv a knife, we have to have it wiv butter, don't we?"[5]

Although Denis is exploring the modal notions of possibility and necessity, which are central to the branch of logic called "modal logic," this anecdote is perhaps prephilosophical rather than philosophical. It doesn't really pose a philosophical problem, let alone attempt to solve one. But it does incorporate the kind of play with concepts that nurtures philosophy.

AFTER WE READ Denis's ruminations at age three years, ten months, on the possibilities and necessities of buttered bread, we are not surprised to find that at age six years he is capable of making remarks that are more clearly philosophical:

> A DISCUSSION about being "early" or "late" for school arose at the breakfast table. James, to his mother, was grumbling about "the fuss people make about getting up early, and things". Denis [six years, one month], with his characteristically slow speech but penetrating thought, said, "Early and late *aren't* things. They're not things like tables and chairs and cups—things you can model!"[6]

Denis's notion of "things like tables and chairs and cups—things you can model" seems to be what many philosophers would call the notion of a material or physical object. Tables, chairs, and cups are material objects; early and late are not.

Of course, "things" in James's expression doesn't mean "material objects." Surely Denis realized this. But he wanted to pretend otherwise. In doing so he could make a little joke that raises interesting conceptual, or philosophical, questions.

The intentional misinterpretation of a form of words is a kind of wordplay that rhetoricians used to call "asteismus."

A good example can be found in act 2, scene 1, of Shakespeare's *Love's Labours Lost:*

Longaville: I desire her name.
Boyet: She hath but one for herself; to desire that were a shame.

An even more obviously philosophical example of asteismus comes from the contemporary playwright Tom Stoppard:

Rosencrantz: We might as well be dead. Do you think Death could possibly be a boat?
Guildenstern: No, no, no ... Death is ... not. Death isn't. You take my meaning. Death is the ultimate negative. Not-being. You can't not-be on a boat.
Rosencrantz: I've frequently not been on boats.
Guildenstern: No, no, no—what you've been is not on boats.[7]

Guildenstern takes from Rosencrantz the virtuoso line "I've frequently not been on boats" and misreads it as a claim about nonbeing, or nonexistence, about, so to speak, doing one's nonexisting on boats. This asteismus thus appeals to the philosophical notion of nonbeing.

Asteismus is endemic to philosophers. That this should be so is not very surprising. Misconstruing a form of words is often an aid to clarifying the logic of a family of expressions and the concepts they express.

Denis's joke with "thing" makes an important point. At times we use "thing" to mean "material or physical object." Thus, we might insist, whereas a cup is a thing, its shape is not a thing, nor is its color. But at other times we use "thing" much more loosely: whatever we can talk about counts as a thing. Because we can talk about shapes and colors (as in "The shape of that cup is pleasing, but the color is not"), we can correctly say that there are such things as shapes and colors.

Denis's remark is open to several interpretations. On one he is denying that early and late are things and is simply giving tables, chairs, and cups as examples of items that are things. On another interpretation he first says that they are not things, and then, having second thoughts, he qualifies his claim to assert that early and late are not things of the type that "you can model," perhaps things that belong to what Aristotle calls the category of substance (of which certain physical objects might be prime examples).

Are things of other types or other categories really things at all? Are, for example, qualities, times, places, events, mental states, or relations between things really things? Augustine was in the grip of that puzzling question when he wrote about stealing pears as a young man:

> I loved nothing in it except the thieving, though I cannot truly speak of that as a thing I could love, and I was only the more miserable because of it . . . Was it then that I also enjoyed the company of those with whom I committed the crime? If this is so, there was something else I loved besides the act of theft; but I cannot call it something else, because companionship, like theft, is not a thing at all. (*Confessions* [trans. R. S. Pine-Coffin] 2.8)

Denis's playful remark might lead one to try to define "thinghood," elucidate the ambiguity of the word "thing," or develop, perhaps in the style of Aristotle, a doctrine of the different categories of things. But it needn't lead anywhere. It is a playfully philosophical remark that can be enjoyed for itself.

ANOTHER irrepressible character in Isaacs's book is Ursula.

> URSULA [three years, four months], "I have a pain in my tummy". Mother, "You lie down and go to sleep and your pain will go away". Ursula, "Where will it go?"[8]

I can't prove that Ursula had a twinkle in her eye when she asked, "Where will it go?" She might have been puzzled, even worried ("Will it go into the closet?" "Will it go under my bed?" "If it goes into the closet, will it come out again while I'm asleep?"). Certainly children do worry about such matters. But because the pattern of anecdotes in Isaacs's book suggests that Ursula was happy, confident, curious, and playful, I suspect that the question was a playful one.

Asked pertly, this question is a teasing invitation to think about pains and about what it is to go away—or better, to think about the various ways in which things do go away. We might first list some of the many things that go away, for example, Grandma, Ursula's dog, a spot on Ursula's dress, a puddle of water, a squeak in Ursula's tricycle.

Grandma and Ursula's dog go away by going to another place. Grandma goes home; the dog goes outdoors. Both may come back by returning from the place to which they have gone. Of course, if Ursula's grandmother or her dog dies, Ursula may be told that her grandmother or dog has "gone away." If the child asks, "Where?" she may be told "To heaven." But in that case, she may be told, the person or animal cannot return to the place where *we* are.

Does a puddle of water go away by going to another place? Not really. Droplets of water evaporate into the sky, but the puddle does not move to the sky.

A spot on Ursula's dress, say, one made by a bit of marmalade at breakfast, may go away when the dress is washed.

It doesn't, however, go away by going to another place. Do its parts go to other places? Perhaps it will disappear altogether.

Most interesting of all, I think, is the squeak in Ursula's tricycle. It may go away when the wheel is oiled. It certainly doesn't go to another place, yet it may come back. If, say, the wheel gets wet again in a rainstorm, the squeak (the very same one!) may come back. For it to come back is not for it to return from a place of hiding, however; rather, it is for the wheel to begin squeaking again in the same way and in the same place.

Of these various things that sometimes go away, squeaks may be most like pains. There are, of course, important differences between pains and squeaks. But just as a squeak goes away when the wheel stops squeaking, so a pain goes away when the tummy stops hurting. Although either may come back, neither returns by coming back from another place.

Ursula's question—"Where will it go?"—is an invitation to philosophical reflection. One can accept the invitation or not, as one chooses. Moreover, one can enjoy the playfulness of the question without pursuing it into reflection.

> URSULA [three years, five months] is continually offering often absurd suggestions about various things: "That *might* be for so-and-so, mightn't it?" and when her mother says, "Yes, but—" she always persists, "But it might, mightn't it?"[9]

Unfortunately, Isaacs provides no sample suggestions. So I have made up these in the spirit of Ursala:

Child: That [table] might be for sitting on, mightn't it?
Adult: Yes, but actually it's for writing on.
Child: But it might, mightn't it?

Child: That [garter] might be for keeping covers on bottles, mightn't it?
Adult: Yes, but actually it's for holding stockings up.
Child: But it might, mightn't it?

The game is of considerable philosophical interest. There is a natural tendency, one firmly embedded in the philosophies of Plato and Aristotle, to understand the nature of a thing by reference to a purpose it serves or might serve. The tendency seems appropriate enough when it is artifacts that we are discussing.

For example, my car has an odd-shaped compartment between the front seats. The compartment itself has an odd-shaped lid and seems designed for a definite purpose, although I can't imagine what it is. I do not know what the compartment is; and not knowing what it is, is the same as not knowing what it is for.

When the tendency to link the nature of a thing with a purpose it might have is carried over to the natural world, scruples arise. Perhaps we can agree that the eye is for seeing and that veins are for returning the blood to the heart. But is the larynx for talking? Is the nose for holding eyeglasses? Are bees for pollinating flowers? Are trees for giving shade, or for preventing erosion? Are rivers for draining excess water from the land and channeling it to the sea, where some of it will evaporate and continue the water cycle?

To say which purposive accounts of things are appropriate and why is a difficult philosophical matter and one of enduring interest. But there is more to Ursula's little game than that. Presumably, Ursula knows that some of her suggested purposes are rather farfetched. By insisting, "But it *might* be for so-and-so, mightn't it?" she is suggesting that there is something indeterminate, even conventional, about what we say things are for. If the purpose of things is to some extent indeterminate or conventional, then, perhaps, so is the nature of things. The thought is as intriguing to some as it is worrying to others. Ursula's game invites us to entertain it.

ANOTHER EXAMPLE is useful for pursuing the idea that philosophy can be play. Suppose that I try using on my son, as I did when he was eight years old, the truism "You can't be in two places at once." And suppose that he replies, as he did, "Yes you can. You can be in the bedroom and in the house at the same time." "But I don't mean that!" I retort with a mixture of pride and annoyance. "So what *do* you mean?" he inquires, grinning mischievously.

The game is to try to give a sense to the truism that will make it come out true. If I say, "I meant two places such that neither is inside the other," he might say, "Well, the bedroom is not in the hallway, and the hallway is not in the bedroom, but you can put one foot in each and be in two places at once." Then I could reply, "I meant *completely* in two places such that neither is inside the other."

At this point we might worry about places, say, the kitchen and the breakfast nook, that overlap. Or John might bring up counterexamples that use "in" in a special way. When, for example, the president talks on television, people say that he is "in" countless homes all over America.

Other counterexamples might highlight peculiar facts of geography. While I was teaching "Philosophy and the Young Child" at the University of Calgary recently, one of my students brought up the interesting case of a town, Lloydminster, that lies directly on the border between Alberta and Saskatchewan. If I am in Lloydminster, am I in both provinces at once? To answer that question, one would need to know whether Lloydminster as a whole is in both provinces or whether the provincial border runs through the town. I am told that the latter is the case. Of course, it could have been otherwise. If the truism "You can't be in two places at the same time" is to be defended against all conceivable counterexamples, it must be interpreted in such a way that it can handle the possibility that Lloydminster as a whole counts as being in both Alberta and Saskatchewan.

MUCH OF WHAT we adults tell children is highly questionable at best and deserves to be challenged. Yet we adults usually turn aside a child's challenge with an irritated "Oh, you know what I mean!" How intimidating, how unfair, how desensitizing that response of annoyance can be! If we ever stopped to reflect seriously and honestly, it might become clear to us that, often enough, there really wasn't anything clear that we could be said to have meant.

It can be fun to play the philosophical game of trying to say what one meant, might have meant, or should have meant when one said something unthinkingly. It can also be enlightening. The logic of containment, the metaphysics of space, or even the geography of Canada may become a little clearer. Parents and teachers who always refuse to play this game with children impoverish their own intellectual lives, diminish their relationships with their children, and discourage in their children the spirit of independent intellectual inquiry.

ANOTHER ANECDOTE from Isaacs's *Intellectual Growth in Young Children* seems to provide a fitting conclusion for this chapter. We see Dan using a classical argument for the beginninglessness of the universe. The spirit is wonderfully engaging through the last joke, which is not only funny but also profound:

> AT LUNCH, the children talked about "the beginning of the world". Dan [six years, one month] insists, whatever may be suggested as "the beginning", there must always have been "something before that". He said, "You see, you might say that first of all there was a stone, and everything came from that—but" (with great emphasis), *"where did the stone come from?"* There were two or three variants on this theme. Then Jane [eleven years], from her superior store of knowledge, said, "Well, I have read that the earth was a piece of the sun, and that the moon was a piece of the earth". Dan, with an air of eagerly pouncing on a fallacy, "Ah! but where did *the sun* come from?" Tommy [five years, four months] who had listened to all this very quietly, now said with a quiet smile, "I know where the sun came from!" The others said eagerly, "*Do* you, Tommy? Where? Tell us". He smiled still more broadly, and said, "Shan't tell you!" to the vast delight of the others, who thoroughly appreciated the joke.[10]

3. Reasoning

LET'S RETURN to Tim and the dream problem. Here is the entire anecdote:

> TIM (about six years), while busily engaged in licking a pot, asked, "Papa, how can we be sure that everything is not a dream?" Somewhat abashed, Tim's father said that he didn't know and asked how Tim thought that we could tell? After a few more licks of the pot, Tim answered, "Well, I don't think everything is a dream, 'cause in a dream people wouldn't go around asking if it was a dream."

In his modern classic, *The Problems of Philosophy*, Bertrand Russell has this to say about Tim's problem:

> There is no logical impossibility in the supposition that the whole of life is a dream, in which we ourselves create all the objects that come before us. But although this is not logically impossible, there is no reason whatever to suppose that it is true; and it is, in fact, a less simple hypothesis, viewed as a means of accounting for the facts of our own life, than the common-sense hypothesis that

there really are objects independent of us, whose action on us causes our sensations.[1]

Tim's problem is different from the other problem of how do I know whether I am now dreaming. This problem, as it is usually conceived, assumes that there are indeed times when we are awake and times when we are dreaming. The question is "How do I know whether I am now awake, or now dreaming?"

Descartes introduces this second problem in an often cited passage in his *Meditations.* He begins by suggesting that he cannot reasonably doubt that he is "here, seated by the fire, wearing a dressing gown, holding this paper in [his] hands." But it occurs to him that he has often dreamt that he was "here, clothed in a dressing gown, and sitting by the fire, although [he] was in fact lying in bed!" Descartes then comments: "When I consider these matters carefully, I realize so clearly that there are no conclusive indications by which waking life can be distinguished from sleep that I am quite astonished, and my bewilderment is such that it is almost able to convince me that I am sleeping."[2]

There is no doubt that the second dream problem is very closely linked in Descartes's own thinking to Tim's problem. The link seems to be this assumption: if there is never a moment at which I can be certain that I am awake, then, for all I know, the distinction I draw between waking life and sleep may be one I draw in a dream and may therefore be as spurious as other illusions of my dreams.

Just before he announces his famous *cogito, ergo sum* ("I think, therefore I am"), Descartes alludes to Tim's problem. However, rather than immediately offer a solution (he does offer one in other places, for example, in his *Sixth Meditation*), Descartes says, in one of the most famous passages in philosophy, that even if all life is no more real than a dream, he can still be sure of his own existence:

> As the same percepts which we have when awake may come to us when asleep without their being true, I decided to suppose that nothing that had ever entered my mind was more real than the illusions of my dreams. But I soon noticed that while I thus wished to think everything false, it was necessarily true that I who thought so was something. Since this truth, *I think, therefore I am, or exist,* was so firm and assured that all the most extravagant suppositions of the sceptics were unable to shake it, I judged that I could safely accept it as the first principle of the philosophy I was seeking.[3]

Is Tim's solution to his dream problem a good one? There can be no doubt that his solution is at least a reasoned one. Here is the reasoning:

(1) If everything were a dream, people wouldn't go around asking if it was a dream.
(2) People do go around asking if it is a dream.
Therefore:
(3) Not everything is a dream.

This argument is certainly valid. That is, the truth of the premises would certainly guarantee the truth of the conclusion. Whether the argument is a good solution to Tim's dream problem depends on whether we have reason to think the premises true. That may not be obvious.

Couldn't one have a dream in which one asks whether one is dreaming? I see no reason why not. Augustine describes a dream in which he tried to convince a man that the man was merely a figment of the dream (*De genesi ad litteram* 12.2.3). Augustine's dream may remind one of this passage from Lewis Carroll's *Through the Looking-Glass:*

> "[The Red King's] dreaming now," said Tweedledee:
> "and what do you think he's dreaming about?"
>
> Alice said "Nobody can guess that."
>
> "Why, about *you!*" Tweedledee exclaimed, clapping
> his hands triumphantly. "And if he left off dreaming
> about you, where do you suppose you'd be?"
>
> "Where I am now, of course," said Alice.
>
> "Not you!" Tweedledee retorted contemptuously.
> "You'd be nowhere. Why, you're only a sort of thing in
> his dream!"
>
> "If that there King was to wake," added Tweedle-
> dum, "you'd go out—bang!—just like a candle!"
>
> "I shouldn't!" Alice exclaimed indignantly. "Besides,
> if *I'm* only a sort of thing in his dream, what are *you,* I
> should like to know?"
>
> "Ditto," said Tweedledum.
>
> "Ditto, ditto!" cried Tweedledee.[4]

Perhaps people who ask questions in dreams aren't really
asking anything, just as, for example, Tweedledum suggests that Alice, because she is in a dream, doesn't cry real
tears. The idea that asking questions in a dream doesn't
really count as asking questions seems to be presupposed by
(1) in Tim's solution. But if we read the last part of (1) in so
strong a way as to require "real" asking, we shall need to
read (2) in a similar manner. And how does Tim know that
anybody is actually asking anything rather than doing so
only in a dream?

I don't want to be too hard on Tim's solution, though. It
could be developed into a sophisticated line of reasoning.[5]
And anyway, neither Descartes's solution nor Russell's is
completely satisfactory.

What is important in the present context is that Tim has
stated a familiar philosophical problem and, in his attempt

to solve it, has provided us with a fine example of philosophical reasoning in a young child.

> SOME QUESTION of fact arose between James and his father, and James said, "I *know* it is!" His father replied, "But perhaps you might be wrong!" Denis [four years, seven months] then joined in, saying, "But if he knows, he can't be wrong! *Thinking*'s sometimes wrong, but *knowing*'s always right!"[6]

Denis is teasing his father, it seems, by appealing to a certain analysis of knowledge, that is, by appealing to some notion of exactly what a claim to know something (say, that P), amounts to. Perhaps the analysis he is appealing to is this one:

> (4) X knows that P if and only if X thinks that P and X cannot be mistaken about whether P.

From this analysis we may infer that

> (5) If James knows that P, then James cannot be mistaken about whether P.

Denis's father doesn't deny that

> (6) James knows that P.

Instead he warns that

> (7) James might be mistaken (about whether P).

Denis seizes on James's claim—"I *know* it is"—which corresponds to (6), and, in effect, deduces from it and (5) the contradictory of (7), namely:

> (8) James can't be mistaken (about whether P).

This, at least, is one plausible reconstruction of what is going on in the anecdote.[7]

Plato, one of the first philosophers to offer an analysis of knowledge, gives us several.[8] According to the one in the *Republic*, knowing is apprehending in such a way that one can't be mistaken about what one believes that one has apprehended (477e). This analysis comes close to (4).

Attempts to provide a satisfactory analysis of knowledge, like attempts to deal with the dream problem, belong to epistemology, the theory of knowledge. Denis's joke, drawing as it does on a familiar analysis of knowledge, is, one might say, an epistemological joke. Moving, as it does, from (5) and (6) to (8), Denis's joke also incorporates reasoning.

> IAN (six years) found to his chagrin that the three children of his parents' friends monopolized the television; they kept him from watching his favorite program. "Mother," he asked in frustration, "why is it better for three people to be selfish than for one?"

As often happens when children ask interesting questions, the mother felt that she did not know how to reply to her son's query. She tucked the question away in her memory. Years later, when I was explaining my interest in philosophical thinking in young children, she recounted the incident and asked whether it might illustrate what I had in mind.

Indeed it does, in its own very special way. Ian, unlike Tim, is not in the grip of philosophical puzzlement. His question, like Denis's comment to his father, is somewhat mischievous. Unlike Denis, however, Ian is making his mischievous point to further a practical end: he wants to watch his favorite television program.

It seems almost certain that Ian was familiar with reasoning that would justify a given act, practice, or social arrangement by appealing to the claim that that act, practice, or arrangement would produce the most happiness. Justifications in ethics that are based on such appeals to what would maximize happiness are called "utilitarian." "Utility" in this context means (perversely, one might think) "happiness." And the principle of utility is the principle that happiness ought always to be maximized.

The principle of utility has enough plausibility for most of us to agree that the question "Why is it better for three people to be happy than for one?" is silly. Ian seems to have latched on to the idea that when X gains what X wants at the expense of Y, then X may be "being selfish." When three people gain what they want—in this case, a chance to watch their favorite television program—at the expense of another's being able to gain what he wants, it may be that the three people are being selfish. Thus, the very same situation that might be justified on the grounds that it maximizes happiness might also be condemned on the grounds that it maximizes selfishness.

To be fair to this situation and to the people involved in it, we would, of course, want to know more details. Did the visiting children realize that in watching their favorite program they were depriving Ian of a chance to watch his? If not, perhaps we shouldn't brand them selfish. On the other hand, maybe they simply did not consider Ian's desires. In that case they could be faulted for lacking moral imagination; perhaps they showed themselves to be self-centered or insensitive rather than selfish. Another possibility is that Ian's mother set things up in such a way that it would have been impolite for the children to question the arrangements, even though they sympathized with Ian.

Whatever the details of the actual situation, we can certainly imagine a case in which all parties involved were aware of each other's preferences and in which the visitors quite happily watched their favorite programs for hours on end knowing that by so doing they were depriving Ian of a chance to enjoy his. It seems that the principle of utility might condone such an arrangement, even enjoin us to preserve it, because doing so would be the moral thing to do in the situation. This possibility seems to expose a major flaw in utilitarianism as a moral theory.

Of course, I do not mean to suggest that Ian, at six years, was consciously trying to refute utilitarianism as an ethical theory. I do mean to suggest, however, that his ingenious reversal of utilitarian reasoning suggests a very interesting and important criticism of the theory.

> A LITTLE GIRL of nine asked: "Daddy, is there really God?" The father answered that it wasn't very certain, to which the child retorted: "There must be really, because he has a name!"[9]

Jean Piaget prefaces this anecdote with the comment that a child's "inability to dissociate names from things is very curious."[10] On first thought there may seem to be nothing paradoxical about the idea of a name without a bearer, but a little reflection easily suggests reasoning that rules out such a possibility:

> The name "Romulus" is not really a name but a sort of truncated description. It stands for a person who did such-and-such things, who killed Remus, and founded Rome, and so on. It is short for that description; if you like, it is short for "the person who was called 'Romulus.' " If it were really a name, the question of existence could not arise, because a name has got to name something or it is not a name, and if there is no such person as Romulus there cannot be a name for that person who is not there.[11]

Boiled down to its essentials, Russell's argument as applied to "Romulus," is exactly the other side of the little girl's argument concerning "God." Russell's argument, or part of it at least, might be put this way:

> (11) If "Romulus" is a name, there exists an entity named "Romulus." ("A name has got to name something or it is not a name.")
> (12) There exists no entity named "Romulus."
> Therefore:
> (13) "Romulus" is not a name.

The little girl's argument, polished just a bit, goes this way:

> (14) If "God" is a name, there exists an entity named "God."
> (15) "God" is a name.
> Therefore:
> (16) There exists an entity named "God."

Both these arguments are valid: they are correct in form. The form of the first argument is traditionally called *modus tollens;* that of the second, *modus ponens.* Whether the arguments give us sufficient reason to accept their conclusions depends on the status of their premises. The principle needed to justify (11) and (14) is, as one might imagine, highly debatable. Issues that surround the acceptance or rejection of that principle lead directly to many of the most fruitful and exciting developments in twentieth-century philosophy.

Piaget was dismissive, even contemptuous, of the little girl's reasoning. He should not have been. It is as old as the pre-Socratic philosopher Parmenides (fifth century B.C.) and as up to date as contemporary discussions of so-called "free logics," nonstandard logics in which "empty" names are allowed.

> JOHN (seven years), thinking that his father had hold of
> his cello, let go of it, and the cello fell over and broke.
> Overcome with remorse (he was very fond of his cello),
> John went to his mother and hugged her quietly for a
> long time. Finally he said, "I wish everything was on a
> film and you could rewind it and do everything over." A
> moment later he added, "Of course, then it would just
> happen again, 'cause there's only one film."

Living in a book culture as we do, it is natural for us to
ask whether there is a "book of life." As the book of life is
usually conceived, the pages of the future are blank. In living our lives—doing this, doing that, making this choice,
making that one—we each write our own book of life.
There could, of course, be a fatalistic version of the book-
of-life idea in which the pages of the future are already
filled; everything that will happen would already be written
there.

Given our modern cinematic culture, an analogy with a
movie film is perhaps more gripping. The fatalistic version
of this analogy concentrates on the projector. According to
it, our lives and experiences unfold with the same inexora-
bility as an unwinding movie film in a cinema. The nonfa-
talistic version centers on the camera. One of the reels in
the camera, the reel of the future, is blank. Only the take-
up reel, the reel of the past, is full.

In this anecdote John is certainly intrigued by a film analogy. What is not so obvious, however, is exactly how he
conceives it.

John must have seen sequences of film run backward on
television; for example, a diver first dives off a board into
the water in the usual way and then, perhaps in apparent
response to the enticement of some advertised refreshment,
rises feet first out of the water and returns to the diving

board in an exact reversal of his earlier trajectory. John was always curious about special effects like this (he liked to perform magic tricks); he certainly knew that film could be reversed to produce such an illusion and then played again in the usual way.

Even more to the point is the rerun on television of a crucial play in a football or baseball game. Again, this is something that John was quite familiar with. Through the miracle of videotape, we can see the crucial play over and over again to study in detail what happened in that crucial moment.

If life were like a film, perhaps John could have run it back to the instant before the cello fell over and broke and, as he said, "do everything over." But a moment's further reflection revealed to John that the possibility of simple re-play would be very uncomforting indeed. (In fact, what it could mean to run the movie of life through a second time is worrisome, unless there were an external observer who could remember having seen it all before.)

Perhaps John was coming to the idea that life is like an already exposed film: everything that is going to happen is already recorded there. In that case, he could no more alter an event by reliving it than he could alter the outcome of a movie by showing the film again. Rather than that fatalistic idea, however, John's idea may have been that the film of life, once exposed, cannot be erased. Or maybe John had in mind something quite different from either of these two possibilities. Perhaps this was his reasoning: Suppose that we ran the film back to the moment before the cello fell. At that point neither John nor I (I am John's father) was worried about the possibility that it would fall. So neither of us would do anything to prevent the accident. Therefore, it would just fall over and break again.

At the time of this incident I was myself too saddened to pursue John's analogy. I cannot now be absolutely sure how he meant the analogy to be taken. Nevertheless, every possibility that I can think of is interesting. And each involves philosophical reasoning.

I RECENTLY taught "Philosophy and the Young Child" in the Harvard Summer School and assigned the usual lab work. One student read a chapter of one of C. S. Lewis's Narnia tales to Michael, then seven years old. A three-hour discussion ensued that covered many of the most philosophical topics imaginable. I was told that the discussion would, in fact, have gone on even longer had Michael's mother not finally appeared to announce that enough was enough.

The discussion began with worries about evil and the origin of evil: "What makes people bad?" "Have people always been bad?" and so on. Talk eventually turned to the universe and its character and finally to whether or not the universe is infinite. My student, I judge, had never before worried seriously about whether the universe is infinite. Michael had: "I don't like to [think] about the universe without an end. It gives me a funny feeling in my stomach. If the universe goes on forever, there is no place for God to live, who made it."

Michael then mentioned an article that his father had written on finite models for the universe. He said that he hadn't read the article and, in effect, didn't want to comment until he had. Yet, unknown to his parents as I later learned, he had turned over in his mind the question as to whether the universe is infinite.

"Why is that important?" asked my student, obviously surprised to find Michael concerned about it.

"It's nice to know you're *here*," replied Michael. "It is not nice to know about nothing. I hope [the universe] doesn't go on and on forever. I don't like the idea of it going on forever because it's obvious it can't be anywhere."

Breathtakingly concise, this bit of reasoning captures what seems to have mattered most to Michael about whether the universe is infinite. An infinite universe can't be located anywhere, nor, as Michael went on to muse, can there be any absolute location *within* an infinite universe.

Michael expressed his thoughts about the last point in terms of the analogy of being lost in a foreign country without the linguistic means of getting one's bearings:

> IT IS LIKE [being] in Japan and no one is English-speaking. No maps and without cash. Only . . . a car. . . . Like being in a big city and not having maps . . . It is nice to know [to] have security to know where you are.

I learned from Michael's mother that shortly before the interview the family had been traveling in France and that they had indeed been lost in a country in which Michael did not speak the language and for which he had no map. Michael's mother had noticed that he was very relieved to get back to England. But she hadn't fully appreciated the emotional impact that the experience of being lost had made on her son. And, of course, she had no idea that the experience had provided for him an analogy for a universe in which there would be no absolute location and thus no way to find out, except in a disappointingly relative fashion, where one is.

Picking up Michael's remarks on insecurity in an infinite universe, my student asked, "What if there is no end? How can we have security? Say we [are] lost in a Chinese city."

"That goes on forever?" Michael asked. "No maps? No

English? [We] would have to try not to crash into cars and drive around like being lost."

"Does finding out if the universe has an end tell us who we are or what we are?" asked my student.

"No," replied Michael, "but it makes us more secure."

"How do we react to space and death?" asked my student later in the discussion.

"It is more important," said Michael firmly, "to know where you are than what happens after you die. Most people don't think about death. It is more important to think about maps in [a] Chinese city than dying. I think I would rather have the maps."

Some adults can, of course, bring much more sophisticated conceptual machinery, including, possibly, noneuclidean geometries, to the consideration of whether the universe is infinite than Michael was able to. But Michael exhibited a clear understanding of some of the basic implications of the question. At times his reasoning was simply stunning. And he definitely had a "gut" sense of the importance of some of the issues that cannot be bettered, I believe, by anyone, adult or child.

Michael is not an entirely typical seven-year-old. Some of his intellectual preoccupations have to do, no doubt, with his mother's being a computer scientist and his father's being a mathematician. Moreover, his willingness to open up to an adult suggests that someone has treated him, as well as what he has to say, with respect.

Though not completely typical, Michael is not, however, entirely atypical either. In fact, such evidence as I have been able to assemble suggests that, for many young members of the human race, philosophical thinking—including, on occasion, subtle and ingenious reasoning—is as natural as making music and playing games, and quite as much a part of being human.

4. Piaget

SOME READERS, no doubt, are wondering whether what I am trying to establish about children and philosophy has not been anticipated by the great Swiss student of intellectual development in young children, Jean Piaget.

Piaget has devoted his professional life to writing on the subject. Some of his best-known work has been devoted to the study of the earliest moves an infant makes toward developing intellectual skills.[1] But Piaget has also concerned himself with later developments. In *The Child's Conception of the World* he addresses a catalogue of obviously philosophical questions: "What is thinking?" "What is the relation between a word and its meaning?" "What are dreams and where are they located?" "What things are alive and what things are conscious?" He asks these questions of youngsters between the ages of five and twelve years. Thus, one might reasonably hope to learn from the book something about philosophical thinking in young children.

Piaget's general technique for charting intellectual devel-

opment is to map three or four stages of progressive sophistication in the mastering of a concept and then to show
that most children of age so-and-so are at Stage I and that
by the time those same chldren are of age such-and-such,
most of them will have reached Stage II and so on.

This procedure raises an initial worry. Is it reasonable to
suppose that children, or anyone else, will make, as a matter
of standard or normal maturation, well-marked progress in
the handling of genuinely philosophical questions? The answer would seem to be "No." The reasons are many. First,
it is notoriously difficult, some would say impossible, for
people to agree on what counts as progress in philosophy.
Second, philosophical progress, measured by any plausible
yardstick, is not a standard development among people in
any age group, whether five to twelve years, twenty-five to
sixty-five years, or whatever.

There is another worry. Piaget proposes to validate his
claims about developmental stages by finding the same patterns of response in all children. Such a finding is to be considered a guarantee that the thinking of children really does
develop in this fashion. The unusual response is discounted
as an unreliable indicator of the ways in which children
think: "The only valid criteria . . . are based on multiplicity
of results and on the comparison of individual reactions."[2]
But it is the deviant response that is most likely to be philosophically interesting. The standard response is, in general,
an unthinking and un-thought-out product of socialization,
whereas the nonconforming response is much more likely
to be the fruit of honest reflection. Yet Piaget would have
the nonconforming response discounted and eliminated on
methodological grounds.

There is yet a further worry. Piaget aims to arrive at
children's convictions. He distinguishes answers and com-

ments that reveal convictions from those that constitute what he calls "mere romancing." Romancing, he explains, is "inventing an answer in which [one] does not really believe, or in which [one] believes merely by force of saying it." Piaget makes clear in a variety of ways that he has little interest in, or appreciation for, romancing. "One would like to be able to rule out romancing," he says gravely, "with the same severity as [the answer intended simply to please the questioner]."[3] (At this point the soft outline of the friendly Swiss psychologist, puffing reflectively on his curved-stem pipe, perceptibly hardens into the stern features of the no-nonsense schoolmaster and disciplinarian.) It seems most likely that the philosophically interesting comments a child makes will not so much express the child's settled convictions as explore a conceptual connection or make a conceptual joke. Thus, the most interesting and intriguing philosophical comments are likely to be counted by Piaget as mere romancing.

Although many of the anecdotes I have already recounted illustrate this point, let me provide a new one.

Once, when my son, John, was six years old, I decided to take him to a concert given by a college orchestra. He was just about to begin taking cello lessons. My thought was to plunk him down in front of the cello section of the orchestra and say, "That instrument is what you are going to play."

When we arrived at the hall where the concert was to be played, we found it dark. The concert had been canceled. Disappointed, we climbed into the car to return home. After I got the car started for the return trip I discovered that a red warning light on the dashboard stayed lighted. My son, sensing that I was worried about something, asked me what was the matter. I explained the function of the warning light: how its staying on was supposed to tell us that the generator wasn't producing enough electricity to keep the battery charged, how we might soon be without lights, and so on.

John reflected for a moment and then piped, "Maybe it's lying!" (An obvious case of romancing.)

I picked up his gauntlet. "I told you there was going to be a concert tonight," I said. "I read in the newspaper that there would be one. But there was no concert. Did I lie to you?"

"No," he said slowly, "the newspaper lied." (More romancing!)

Well, we had something to discuss for the trip home. Slowly and carefully, we analyzed the concept of lying. Eventually, after several missteps, we came to the conclusion that to lie you must intend to deceive someone else; so you yourself must know that what you are saying is false. (I deliberately avoided the possibility of self-deception, lying to oneself. I look forward to the day when John and I can discuss that!)

"Do you think," I asked triumphantly as we put the car in the garage, "that the light might have *known* that what it was telling us was false?"

"No."

"Why not?"

"It hasn't got a brain."

I was pleased.

Then came the parting shot. "Okay, it wasn't lying," agreed my son, "but maybe it was just teasing." (Inveterate romancer!)

That last move was a good one. Analyzing the concept of teasing would postpone bedtime indefinitely. I was tempted to go on, but not quite strongly enough. Instead of analyzing the concept of teasing with my young philosopher, I heartlessly hustled him off to bed.

No exchange like this one appears in Piaget's book. What Piaget says about romancing suggests that he would have discouraged a discussion in such a style. In discouraging it, however, he discourages philosophy.

What, then, does Piaget count as progress in concept formation? And how does he think it can be detected?

In the first chapter of *The Child's Conception of the World* Piaget outlines his procedure:

> The technique is briefly as follows. The child is asked: "Do you know what it means to think of something? When you are here and you think of your house, or when you think of the holidays, or of your mother, you are thinking of something." And then when the child has understood: "Well then, what is it you think with?" If, as seldom happens, he has not grasped the idea, the matter must be further explained: "When you walk, you walk with the feet; well then, when you think, what do you think with?" Whatever the answer may be, the meaning behind the words is what matters. Finally comes the question, supposing it were possible to open a person's head without his dying, could you see a thought, or touch it, or feel it with the finger, etc. Naturally, these last questions, which are suggestive, must be kept to the end, that is to say till the moment when the child cannot be made to say anything more of itself.[4]

Piaget claims to detect three stages of increasing sophistication in the development of the child's notion of thinking and tries to distinguish them:

> During [the first] stage children believe that thinking is "with the mouth". Thought is identified with the voice. Nothing takes place in the head or in the body . . .

There is nothing subjective in the act of thinking. The average age for children of this stage is 6.

The second stage is marked by adult influences. The child has learnt that we think with the head, sometimes it even alludes to the "brain" . . . This type of answer is always found about the age of 8. But more important is the continuity existing between the first and second stages. Indeed, thought is often looked on as a voice inside the head, or in the neck, which shows the persistence of the influence of the child's previous convictions. Finally, there is the way in which the child materialises thought: thought is made of air, or of blood, or it is a ball, etc.

The third stage, the average age of which is 11–12, shows thought no longer materialised.[5]

Anyone familiar with classical theories of thinking will be able to link them with Piaget's three stages. The idea that thinking is inner speech is to be found in Plato's works, for example, in this passage from his dialogue "Theaetetus":

Socrates: Do you accept my description of the process of thinking?

Theaetetus: How do you describe it?

Socrates: As a discourse that the mind carries on with itself about any subject it is considering. You must take this explanation as coming from an ignoramus [someone stuck at Stage I, perhaps!]; but I have a notion that, when the mind is thinking, it is simply talking to itself, asking questions and answering them, and saying Yes or No. When it reaches a decision—which may come slowly or in a sudden rush—when doubt is over and the two voices affirm the same thing, then we call that its "judgment". So I should describe thinking as discourse, and judgment as a statement pronounced, not aloud to someone else, but silently to oneself.

(Trans. F. M. Cornford, 189e–190a)

Plato's theory has been revived and modified in modern times. The analogical theory of judgment in P. T. Geach's *Mental Acts* is one modern version. Quite a different version, but one much more in line with Piaget's Stage I, is to be found in the writings of the behaviorist psychologist J. B. Watson. According to Watson's theory, children are conditioned to inhibit their vocal speech by adults who are tired of hearing endless infant chatter. In response to admonitions to keep quiet, children first mumble and finally so inhibit their speech that they make no audible sound and no movement of the lips. All they do is move the muscles of their mouth and throat. This inhibited, or subvocal, speech, says Watson, is thinking.[6]

Corresponding to Piaget's second stage are various materialistic theories of thinking, including what today is called "the identity theory." Thought is not considered to be "made of air, or of blood" or to be a ball, but, in supposing mental events to be identical with brain events, the identity theorist certainly "materializes thought." To judge from the space devoted to the defense and criticism of the identity theory in current philosophy journals, this kind of account offers the most exciting contemporary approach to the old problem of what thinking is.

Finally, the third stage in Piaget's classification corresponds to classical dualistic theories, especially imagistic accounts in the empiricist tradition. Perhaps the long and fascinating chapter "The Stream of Thought" in William James's *The Principles of Psychology* gives the fullest, most vivid exposition of this sort of view.[7]

We might, of course, question whether Piaget's sample or his method of conducting research justifies his conclusion that children naturally develop ideas about thinking in this particular sequence. But suppose that we were satisfied with those aspects of Piaget's research. The notion of progress built into his methodology would still be worth worrying about.

It is characteristic of the first stage, Piaget says, for the child to think that "there is nothing subjective in the act of thinking." Piaget makes clear that in his view this is a deficiency in the child's notion of thought, a deficiency to be corrected at a later stage. About the first stage Piaget also says: "In treating of the development of the notion of thought, we may regard as primitive the child's conviction that it thinks with the mouth. The notion of thinking, as soon as it appears, becomes confused with that of voice, that is to say with words, either spoken or heard."[8]

The implication seems to be that a philosopher like Geach who tries to develop an account of thinking as inner speech is retarded, or unnaturally arrested, in his intellectual development. All the more so if that philosopher or psychologist (I have Watson in mind) persists in supposing, even insists on supposing, that "there is nothing subjective in the act of thinking." Identity theorists have at least progressed beyond the first stage. But, to judge from Piaget's schedule of natural development, their progress is also unnaturally arrested.

"Hold on!" you may protest. "This is all melodramatic and overdrawn. Piaget does not claim that a normal six-year-old holds, say, a behavioristic theory of thinking, whereas an eight-year-old standardly holds an identity theory and a twelve-year-old a dualistic theory. Piaget doesn't suppose that any of these children has developed, or would even understand, a *theory* of what thinking is. It's just that when you ask a six-year-old the question 'What do you think with?' you can expect to get the answer 'With my mouth,' whereas two years later you can expect the answer 'With my head,' 'With my brian,' or something similar."

It is, no doubt, true that Piaget does not attribute theories of thinking to his subjects. To say that someone accepts a particular theory is to suggest that that person has well-worked-out answers to a range of questions concerning the subject of the theory. Piaget expects that his subjects will often be stumped by simple questions about thinking and that their answers will sometimes be incoherent.

So Piaget doesn't really suppose that his subjects subscribe to theories such as behaviorism, dualism, and materialism. On the other hand, however, it isn't right either to say that he simply collects and tabulates responses to such questions as "What do you think with?" (for example, X percent of respondents of age Y answered, "With the mouth"). Rather, Piaget is interested in the child's conception of the world and thus in the child's conception of what thought is. We are to go behind the child's words to what they reveal about the child's conceptual world. Granted, to suggest that the child has a *theory* of what a thought is may be too grandiose. But Piaget certainly supposes that the child has, even at age six years, a *concept* of thinking. (After all, his chapter is entitled "The Notion of Thought.")

Piaget makes his intent reasonably clear in the following passage from his opening, methodological chapter:

> An attempt must be made to strip the answers of their verbal element. There is certainly present to the child a whole world of thought, incapable of formulation and made up of images and motor schemas combined. Out of it issue, at least partially, ideas of force, life, weight, etc., and the relations of objects amongst themselves are penetrated with these indefinable associations. When the

child is questioned he translates his thought into words, but these words are necessarily inadequate.[9]

So it is the child's conceptual world, to which the child's own words are "necessarily inadequate," that Piaget is interested in. And so it is conceptions of thought, for example, that Piaget means to deal with. The sequence of conceptions of thought that he claims to find in children from ages five through twelve years parallels, as we discover, a list of classical theories of thinking.

We thus return to the initial embarrassment. Can it be that Piaget supposes a behaviorist to be someone whose conception of thought has never advanced beyond Stage I? Or does he suppose that a behaviorist, say, first makes progress through childhood and adolescence and then, in adult life, regresses to Stage I?

We might try to get Piaget out of this embarrassment by playing down the idea of progress. It might be that all he means to be pointing out is that conceptions of thinking, dreaming, meaning, life, and so on change in identifiable patterns. Perhaps he is not, in fact, committed to viewing this sequence as a line of progress. If he is not, then perhaps there is no embarrassment after all in finding an adult, even a learned philosopher or psychologist, whose view of thinking corresponds to that of a six-year-old or an eight-year-old.

Unfortunately, this way out does not fit the text. Piaget makes clear throughout his book that the story of conceptual change he tells is a story of successively closer approximation to adequacy. A passage from the chapter summarizing his discussions of the child's concepts of thinking, meaning, and dreaming provides a good example:

The distinction between thought and the external world is not innate in the child but is only gradually evolved and built up by a slow process. One result of this is of primary importance to the study of causality, namely that the child is a realist and that its progress consists in ridding itself of this initial realism. In fact, during the primitive stages, since the child is not yet conscious of his subjectivity, all reality appears to be of one unvaried type by reason of the confusion between the data of the external world and those of the internal. Reality is impregnated with self and thought is conceived as belonging to the category of physical matter.[10]

As I read these words, there beat in on me the words of my teacher W. V. Quine, spoken to me when I was a graduate student. We were discussing whether the element of what philosophers call "intentionality," that hallmark of the "inner" and the nonphysical, could be eliminated from reports of what someone is thinking. I was skeptical, Quine insistent. "Let's face it, Matthews," he said earnestly, "it's one world and it's a *physical* world."

Back to Piaget.

There are thus two forms of egocentricity, the first logical and the second ontological. Just as the child makes his own truth, so he makes his own reality; he feels the resistance of matter no more than he feels the difficulty of giving proofs. He states without proof and he commands without limit. Magic on the ontological plane, and conviction without proof on the logical ... At the root both of magic and of conviction without proof lie the same egocentric illusions, namely, confusion between one's own thought and that of others and confusion between the self and the external world.[11]

Piaget seems not to have left us any good way of getting him out of the embarrassment of suggesting that behaviorists and identity theorists are retarded children.

There is something else unsettling about these last remarks of Piaget's. Taken seriously, they suggest that it would be folly to try to talk philosophy with a child and capricious and unreasonable to expect a child to say anything philosophically interesting. They imply that a child develops a conception of the world oblivious to the legitimate constraints of logic and experience. The unspoken assumption is that, by contrast, "we" adults are properly respectful of logic and experience.

Surely Piaget's low regard for the thinking of young children is unwarranted. I have already presented considerable evidence to that effect. However, to see that some children can hold their own philosophically with Piaget, we need look no further than some of the interrogatories in his own book. Although many of these exchanges are quoted in such an abbreviated form that it is hard to base much upon them, some are reported at length. One is a fascinating exchange with an eight-year-old:

> Fav . . . belongs to a class whose teacher follows the excellent practice of giving each child an "observation notebook", in which the child notes down each day, with or without the help of drawings, an event he has personally observed outside school. One morning Fav noted down, as always, spontaneously: "I dreamt that the devil wanted to boil me", and he accompanied the observation with a drawing, of which we give a reproduction: on the left Fav is seen in bed, in the centre is the devil and on the right Fav stands, in his nightshirt, in front of the devil who is about to boil him. Our attention was called to this drawing and we sought out Fav. His drawing il-

lustrates very clearly the meaning of child realism: the dream is beside the bed, before the eyes of the dreamer who watches it. Fav, moreover, is in his nightshirt in the dream, as if the devil had pulled him out of bed.

The following are the observations we made: concerning the origin of dreams, Fav has passed the beliefs of the first stage. Like Schi, he knows that the dream comes from thought:

"What is a dream?

It is a thought.

Where does it come from?

When you see something and then you think of it.

Do we make the dream ourselves?

Yes.

Does it come from outside?

No." Fav also knows that we think *"with the brain, with our intelligence."* Further, Fav, like Schi and all the children of this stage, knows that he alone can see his dream; neither we nor anyone else could have seen the dream of the devil in Fav's room. But what he has not understood is the internal nature of the dream:

"While you are dreaming, where is the dream?
In front of the eyes.
Where?
When you are in bed, in front of your eyes.
Where, quite near?
No, in the room." We pointed to Fav's portrait of himself, which we have marked II.
"What is that?
That's me.
Which is most real of you, this (I) or that (II)?
In the dream (pointing to II).
Is this one anything (II)?
Yes, it's me. It was specially my eyes which stayed there (pointing to I) *to see.* (!)
How were your eyes there?
I was there altogether, but specially my eyes.
And the rest of you?
It was there too (in the bed).
How could that be?
There were two of me. I was in my bed and I was looking on all the time.
With the eyes open or shut?
Shut, because I was asleep." A moment later it seemed as if Fav had understood the internal nature of the dream:
"When you are asleep, is the dream in you or are you in the dream?
The dream is in us, because it's we who see the dream.
Is it inside the head or outside?
In the head.
Just now you said outside, what does that mean?
You can't see the dream on the eyes.
Where is the dream?

In front of the eyes.
Is there really anything in front of the eyes?
Yes.
What?
The dream."Fav thus realises there is something internal about the dream, he knows the dream's appearance of externality to be illusion ("you can't see the dream on the eyes"), and yet he admits that for the illusion to be there, there must really be something in front of him:

"Were you really there (pointing to II)?
Yes, I was there twice over (I and II).
If I had been there (II), should I have seen you?
No.
What do you mean by "I was there twice over?"
When I was in bed I was really there, and then when I was in my dream I was with the devil, and I was really there as well."[12]

(I shall assume that it was Piaget himself who conducted this discussion with Fav.)

Clearly, Piaget's overriding interest is to determine whether Fav still has a second-stage concept of dreaming or whether he has moved on to Stage III. Piaget characterizes the two stages this way:

> During the second stage (average age 7–8) the child supposes the source of the dream to be in the head, in thought, in the voice, etc., but the dream is in the room, in front of him. Dreaming is with the eyes; it is looking at a picture outside ... During the third stage (about 9–10), the dream is the product of thought, it takes place inside the head (or in the eyes), and dreaming is by means of thought or else with the eyes, used internally.[13]

I'm not at all sure that I understand the characterization of these two stages. Common to them is supposed to be the idea that the dream is "produced internally" (whatever that means). The difference is supposed to be that, whereas in the second stage a child believes the dream to be "in the room, in front of him," in the third stage the child supposes that it "takes place [not in the room but] inside the head (or in the eyes)."

So the question is "Where does Fav think the dream is, in the room or in his head?" Piaget takes the two figures of Fav in the picture to betray an ambivalence in Fav; they suggest that he is halfway between Stage II and Stage III, Piaget supposes.

For himself, Fav wants to say both these things:

    (1) Throughout the dream I was in my bed asleep.
    (2) Throughout the dream I was outside the bed, in the room.

He seems to realize that, given certain natural assumptions, the two are incompatible. In particular, given the assumption that one person can't be in two places at once (of course, before relying too heavily on that "truism," it might be well to recall my game with John), Fav can't be at once in bed and out in the room. Fav's solution is to multiply himself: "There was two of me . . . I was there twice over."

Another solution would be to say that the expression "throughout the dream" in (1) and (2) is ambiguous. If it is taken to mean "in the whole of the dream," then (2) is true and (1) false. If it is taken to mean "for the whole period of time in which I had the dream," then (1) is true and (2) false.

Actually, the second solution is not very good. For if one dreams about the very period of time during which one is asleep, then one is again forced to conclude that, say, at two in the morning one was both in bed and standing up in the room.

Piaget's solution seems to be simply to deny (2) and replace it with something like this:

> Throughout the dream I *seemed* to myself to be outside the bed, in the room.

That is, "he knows the dream's appearance of externality to be illusion."

So far, the move is a good one. But Piaget is so preoccupied with what he calls the "internal nature of the dream" that he puts the question "When you are asleep, is the dream in you or are you in the dream?" to Fav and in such a way as to make clear that in his view

(3) The dream is in Fav

is true, but

(4) Fav is in the dream

is false. Fav is happy enough to accept (3), but he refuses to give up, and quite rightly so, (4). After all, it was *his* dream and he knows that he was in it.

In this episode Piaget is given a chance to do some philosophy with a child but passes it by. His only interest in talking with Fav seems to be to place the child somewhere on the scale of dream competence.

To me the most striking aspect of this exchange is Piaget's seeming insensitivity to puzzlement. How can anybody ask anybody else, adult or child, "Were you in the dream or was the dream in you?" and not succumb to some degree of puzzlement over the naturalness, given a dream with analogous content, of the answer "Both—I was in the dream and the dream was in me." Fav is puzzled. Piaget isn't.

We have a clue as to how Piaget can treat an inner-speech concept of thinking and a materialistic concept of thinking as mere stages in a child's intellectual development. It doesn't occur to him that what he takes to be the adult concept of thought generates problems or puzzles or perplexities. Not having treated the "earlier" conceptions reflectively, he is not prepared to treat the "adult" conception reflectively either. So, from the point of view of his story of intellectual development, it becomes completely mysterious why adults should revert to the concepts of their youth.

In fact, all the concepts that Piaget claims to have found in children invite philosophical reflection. Moreover, that his third-stage notions are generally more nearly adequate or satisfactory than his first- or second-stage notions isn't at all obvious.

Some people are immune to philosophical puzzlement. For them there is, perhaps, much to learn about the world but nothing to puzzle over. To judge from *The Child's Conception of the World*, Piaget is himself such a person. For someone like me, by contrast, someone who still finds puzzling a great many things about thinking, meaning, dreaming, life, consciousness—the topics of Piaget's book—a child's remark or a drawing like Fav's can start a little colloquy, with the child or with oneself, in which one tries to reason one's way out of the puzzle.

Consider Fav's drawing. Fav appears in the drawing, as he says, "twice over." In a way it seems quite right that he should. After all, he was in his bed the whole time he had the dream and he was also, again for the whole dream, outside the bed, standing on the other side of the devil. But can anybody be in two places at once?

That philosophy can begin with a child in so simple a way says something important about philosophy, and something important about children. It is something that Piaget has missed.

5. Stories

IF PIAGET, the first great psychologist of cognitive development and perhaps the only great one, isn't sensitive to philosophical thinking in young children, who is?[1] Not, in general, other developmental psychologists. Nor, I think, educational theorists. Who then?

The answer may come as a surprise. It is writers—at least some writers—of children's stories who have been almost the only important adults to recognize that many children are naturally intrigued by philosophical questions.

Consider *The Bear That Wasn't,* which begins:

> Once upon a time, in fact it was on a Tuesday, the Bear stood at the edge of a great forest and gazed up at the sky. Away up high, he saw a flock of geese flying south. Then he gazed up at the trees of the forest. The leaves had turned all yellow and brown and were falling from the branches. He knew when the geese flew south and the leaves fell from the trees, that winter would soon be here and snow would cover the forest. It was time to go into a cave and hibernate. And that was just what he did.[2]

As the story continues, the environment over the Bear's cave is transformed. Workers come "with charts and maps and surveying instruments." What they do is chart, map, and survey—"all over the place." Then more workers come; they have "steamshovels and saws and tractors and axes." What they do is steamshovel, saw, tractor, and ax—"all over the place."

What finally emerges from all this frantic activity is "a great, big, huge, factory, right OVER the TOP of the sleeping Bear's cave." In fact, the factory begins to operate before the Bear awakens in the spring.

When the Bear does awaken, he dreamily reorients himself to his cave and its entrance. Sleepily, he makes his way to the entrance and out "into the spring sunshine." A "shock" scene follows:

> His eyes were only half opened, as he was still very sleepy. His eyes didn't stay half opened long. They suddenly POPPED wide apart. He looked straight ahead.
> Where was the forest?
> Where was the grass?
> Where were the trees?
> Where were the flowers?
> WHAT HAD HAPPENED? Where was he?

The factory scene that the Bear looks out on is so completely different from what his memory has led him to expect that he concludes that he must be dreaming:

> "I must be dreaming," he said. "Of course that's it, I'm dreaming." So he closed his eyes and pinched himself. Then he opened his eyes very slowly and looked about. The big buildings were still there. It wasn't a dream. It was real.

It's easy to appreciate the Bear's astonishment. Who wouldn't be astonished? But it's hard to take seriously the Bear's procedure for determining whether he is dreaming.

Though hard, it is not impossible. At least one philosopher, John O. Nelson, has argued that the procedure the Bear uses is effective.[3]

Yet surely this procedure is unreliable; surely it won't work. If the Bear doesn't know whether he is awake, then he doesn't know either, presumably, whether he is really pinching himself or only dreaming that he is.

Would some other procedure be better? Is there a serious, workable method for determining whether one is awake or dreaming?

Frank Tashlin, the author of the story, never supplants his whimsical procedure for determining whether one is dreaming with anything more serious. The dream test, however, is not the only philosophical angle to his story.

The story's very title bespeaks a philosophical sensibility. The "wasn't" in *The Bear That Wasn't* hovers nicely between an intransitive complete use ("wasn't" = "didn't exist") and an intransitive copulative use ("wasn't" = "wasn't such-and-such," for example, "wasn't a bear" or "wasn't what it was thought to be"). One scholar has suggested that it is with just such a hovering between complete and incomplete uses of the verb "to be" that the pre-Socratic philosopher Parmenides inaugurated philosophical discussion of nonbeing.[4]

In Tashlin's story the Factory Foreman, the General Manager, the Third Vice-President, the Second Vice-President, the First Vice-President, and the President of the Factory all insist that the creature before them is not a bear. Instead, they say, he is a "silly man who needs a shave and wears a fur coat." They want him to get back to work. If all these people are right, if what stands before them is not a bear, then it is an illusion and there really is no such bear as the one the story has supposedly been telling us about.

As the story progresses, the Bear himself begins to lose confidence that he is a bear. Is it that he once knew that he was a bear and now doesn't? What was the basis for his former knowledge, and what now calls that basis into question? If he never really had good reason to think that he was a bear, could he be properly said to have known that he was? How much basis does any of us have for knowing what we commonly say and think we know? The taunts of the zoo bears—"No, he isn't a Bear, because if he were a Bear, he wouldn't be outside the cage with you; he would be inside the cage with us"—remind us of the inane conventionality that underlies so many of our claims to knowledge.

The philosophical themes that emerge in *The Bear That Wasn't* thus include at least these four: dreaming and skepticism; being and nonbeing; appearance and reality; and the foundations of knowledge.

Of course, I don't mean to suggest that *The Bear That Wasn't* is a philosophical treatise, even a philosophical treatise in disguise. It isn't a work in philosophy at all. It's a children's story. But its style, which I call "philosophical whimsy," consists in raising, wryly, a host of basic epistemological and metaphysical questions familiar to students of philosophy. Although *The Bear That Wasn't* is an especially good example of philosophical whimsy, that style of writing is not at all unusual in children's literature.

ANOTHER MASTER of philosophical whimsy is L. Frank Baum, author of the popular *The Wonderful Wizard of Oz.*[5] Although some of Baum's other books offer perhaps better examples of philosophical whimsy than the

Wizard does, there is at least one passage in the *Wizard* that illustrates wonderfully the kind of whimsy I have in mind: the autobiography of the Tin Woodman.

As readers of unexpurgated Baum know, the Woodman began life as a creature of flesh and bones. He was gradually transformed by the successive amputation and tin replacement of each limb and gross segment of his body until, in the end, he was all tin. His life story parallels one version of the familiar fable of the ship of Theseus, whose boards were replaced one at a time until there were all new ones. As with the ship of Theseus, the problem is to say when during the process of piece-by-piece replacement, and why then, the original entity ceases to exist.[6]

The Tin Woodman's story, however, adds two elements to the familiar puzzle about piece-by-piece replacement. One is that the Woodman receives tin parts for parts of flesh and bones. (For the ship of Theseus, of course, wood replaces wood). The change in the kind of material—especially when the original, flesh and bones, is so closely linked with the kind of being that the original entity is—affects our intuitions about whether anything survives the transformation. A tin creature seems to have less claim to being a man (I am assuming that the Munchkins in the story are human beings), and hence less claim to being the *same* man, than would a creature composed entirely of "fleshy transplants." (But what about plastic, especially the type that simulates flesh and bones?)

The second new element is the Tin Woodman's memory. The ship of Theseus can't, of course, remember anything. The Tin Woodman, by contrast, tells the story of gradual transformation as the story of his life. Ever since John Locke first proposed memory as a criterion for personal identity, philosophers have taken memory very seriously in discussing these matters.[7]

A THIRD MASTER of philosophical whimsy in children's literature is James Thurber. In his delightful *Many Moons* Thurber describes the efforts of a king to nurse his daughter Lenore to health by fulfilling her wish to have the moon. "If I can have the moon," she tells the King, "I will be well again."[8] Unfortunately for the King, not the Lord High Chamberlain nor the Royal Wizard nor the Royal Mathematician can help the King grant Princess Lenore's request. The King flies into a rage, and then falls into despair. Only the Court Jester thinks to ask the Princess Lenore how big she thinks the moon is, and how far away:

> "How big do you think [the moon] is?"
> "It is just a little smaller than my thumbnail," she said, "for when I hold my thumbnail up at the moon, it just covers it."
> "And how far away is it?" asked the Court Jester.
> "It is not as high as the big tree outside my window," said the Princess, "for sometimes it gets caught in the top branches."

On hearing these answers the Court Jester has the Royal Goldsmith make "a tiny round golden moon just a little smaller than the thumbnail of the Princess Lenore" and string it on a golden chain.

Puzzling over the apparent size of objects seen from a great distance (as when John Edgar wondered whether things get smaller in airplanes as they go up into the sky) seems to be fairly common in children. Two anecdotes about Ursula (who has already been introduced) raise the same sort of question:

> COMING DOWN the mountain, as the train went through a small tunnel, from where they sat Ursula [three years, six months] and her parents got a very good view of the perspective of the round exit of the tube through which they were to go. Ursula said, "Oh, look. It looks very weeny. Why does it?"
>
> On the Rigi Kulm, looking at the Bernese Oberland panorama, Ursula's father pointed to the Jungfrau and said, "There's a house up there". Ursula [three years, six months], "How could anyone live up there, so weeny".[9]

The philosophically smug reader of *Many Moons*—it may well be the parent rather than the child—will simply smile at the Princess Lenore's naiveté and turn to other matters. But for the more reflective mind, Thurber's beautiful story will raise a clutch of questions about perception, illusion, apparent size, and apparent distance that have intrigued philosophers for twenty-five hundred years.[10]

A FOURTH EXAMPLE of philosophical whimsy is A. A. Milne's *Winnie-the-Pooh.* In one passage Rabbit is explaining his plan to capture Baby Roo. When Kanga asks, "Where's Baby Roo?" the others are to say, "Aha!"

> "*Aha!*" said Pooh, practising. "*Aha! Aha!* ... Of course," he went on, "we could say 'Aha!' even if we hadn't stolen Baby Roo."
>
> "Pooh," said Rabbit kindly, "you haven't any brain."
>
> "I know," said Pooh humbly.
>
> "We say '*Aha!*' so that Kanga knows that *we* know where Baby Roo is. '*Aha!*' means 'We'll tell you where

Baby Roo is, if you promise to go away from the Forest and never come back.' Now don't talk while I think."

Pooh went into a corner and tried saying *"Aha!"* in that sort of voice. Sometimes it seemed to him that it did mean what Rabbit said, and sometimes it seemed to him that it didn't. "I suppose it's just practise," he thought. "I wonder if Kanga will have to practise too to understand it."[11]

The idea that a word can be made to mean just what we want it to mean might be called the "Humpty Dumpty theory of meaning," after a famous passage from Lewis Carroll's *Through the Looking-Glass:*

"There's glory for you!"

"I don't know what you mean by 'glory,' " Alice said.

Humpty Dumpty smiled contemptuously. "Of course you don't—till I tell you. I meant 'there's a nice knock-down argument for you!' "

"But 'glory' doesn't mean a 'nice knock-down argument,' " Alice objected.

"When I use a word," Humpty Dumpty said, in rather a scornful tone, "it means just what I choose it to mean—neither more nor less."

"The question is," said Alice, "whether you *can* make words mean so many different things."

"The question is," said Humpty Dumpty, "which is to be master—that's all.[12]

What gives the Humpty Dumpty theory its plausibility is the very natural notion that the meaning a word has when it is used on a particular occasion is the idea or mental picture that the speaker or writer had in mind when the word was uttered or written.

Ludwig Wittgenstein, in his *Philosophical Investigations,* devotes considerable attention to the Humpty Dumpty theory and to the ideas about thinking and meaning that naturally go with it. In this brief passage he rejects the theory: "Can I say 'bububu' and mean 'If it doesn't rain I shall go for a walk'?—It is only in a language that I can mean something by something. This shews clearly that the grammar of 'to mean' is not like that of the expression 'to imagine' and the like."[13]

FOR A FIFTH EXAMPLE of philosophical whimsy in children's literature I turn to a splendid collection of stories by Arnold Lobel entitled *Frog and Toad Together*. Many of Lobel's stories, in this collection and elsewhere, make wry comments on language, life, and human nature. One of my favorites is "Cookies." It goes this way.

Frog and Toad begin eating cookies that Toad has baked. They eat and eat until Frog, with his mouth full of cookies, finally says, "I think we should stop eating. We will soon be sick." Toad agrees, but wants to eat one last cookie; they do. Then they eat one *very* last cookie. Frog says that what they need is willpower. To Toad's question "What is will power?" Frog answers, "Will power is trying hard *not* to do something that you really want to do." Frog puts the remaining cookies in a box and announces that they will eat no more. "But we can open the box," says Toad. "That's true," admits Frog. Frog gets a ladder and puts the box on a high shelf. "But we can climb the ladder," Toad points out. Finally, in desperation, Frog goes outside and gives the remaining cookies to the birds. "Now we have no more cookies to eat," says Toad sadly. "Not even one." "Yes," says Frog, "but we have lots and lots of will power."[14]

The notion of the will and the associated notion of will-power are philosophically both vexed and vexing. Some of the vexations have to do with the idea of determinism and whether determinism is compatible with free will. Others have to do with the idea of weakness of will or lack of willpower.

Frog says that willpower is "trying hard *not* to do something you really want to do." There is something very puzzling about the idea of trying *not* to do what you really want to do. If you really want to do a thing, you won't try *not* to. On the other hand, if you really try not to, it will be because you want not to do it. Thus, what Frog describes as a lack of willpower—indeed, what we all do—begins to look like a case of conflicting desires. Toad wants to stop; but he also, and even more strongly, wants to continue eating cookies.

At this point it is easy to think of Toad as a collection of desires, including the desire to stop eating cookies (not very strong just now) and the desire to continue (very strong). Suppose that Toad continues to eat cookies. Who is to blame? The desire to stop, for being too weak? Or the desire to continue, for being too strong? Or is it silly to blame a desire for being too strong or too weak? A desire, it may seem, is as strong as it is, and that's the end of the matter.

When Saint Paul says, "Now if I do what I do not want, it is no longer I that do it, but sin that dwells within me" (Rom. 7:20), he seems to be identifying himself with his good desires and disowning the others as an alien, subversive force (sin). But isn't the man, Saint Paul, as much the bad impulses as the good ones? As much the id as the superego?

Lobel's gentle and loving mockery of Frog and Toad invites us to reflect on the phenomenon of weakness of will and to join philosophers from Aristotle to the present in trying to understand it (see *Nichomachean Ethics*, bk. 7). The phenomenon is as familiar as it is difficult to be clear about.

6. Fantasy

ALL THE STORIES in the last chapter are examples of fantasy in children's literature. Bruno Bettelheim, in his recent, well-received *The Uses of Enchantment: The Meaning and Importance of Fairy Tales,* argues eloquently that fantasy is important in the development of a young child.[1] Has Bettelheim also recognized the role that stories can play in stimulating philosophical thinking in young children?

The answer is "No"—a resounding "No." To see why, consider the following claims:

1. To the primitive man the sun is alive because it gives light; the stream is alive, and has a will, because its water flows.

2. Realistic explanations are usually incomprehensible to the primitive because he lacks the abstract understanding required to make sense of them.

3. The way true stories about the real world unfold is as alien to the way the mind of the primitive functions as the supernatural events of the fairy tale are to the way the mind of a civilized person functions.

4. The primitive alternates between moods of utter despair and perfect bliss. Either he is in the darkest hell of gloom or he is gloriously happy; there is no in-between.

5. One might rightly question the eighteenth-century belief in the innocence of the primitive, but certainly the idea of showing mercy to the unjust, characteristic of the civilized mind, baffles the primitive.

Suppose that one accepted these claims. What sort of attitude would acceptance encourage?

One might, of course, become fascinated with the societies and cultures of primitive peoples. It is both puzzling and fascinating to think that other peoples might be as different from us as these claims make out. But surely one wouldn't expect to be able to communicate very well with primitive peoples, at least not without a long period of adjusting to their ways. Most important, it would be quite natural to view primitive peoples and their societies and cultures with condescension. If "true stories about the real world" are "alien to the way the mind of the primitive functions" and "the idea of showing mercy to the unjust . . . baffles the primitive," then primitives are obviously to be pitied (and perhaps also to be feared!).

I hope that it will shock my readers to learn that the five claims about the primitive are almost exactly the claims that Bettelheim makes about the child. I have, in fact, taken them from *The Uses of Enchantment,* only turning what Bettelheim says about children into claims about primitives:

[1.] To the eight-year-old (to quote Piaget's examples), the sun is alive because it gives light (and, one may add, it does that because it wants to). To the child's animistic mind, the stone is alive because it can move, as it rolls down a hill. Even a twelve-and-a-half-year-old is convinced that a stream is alive and has a will, because its water is flowing.

[2.] Realistic explanations are usually incomprehensible to children, because they lack the abstract understanding required to make sense of them.

[3.] The way ["true" stories about the "real" world] unfold is as alien to the way the prepubertal child's mind functions as the supernatural events of the fairy tale are to the way the mature intellect comprehends the world.

[4.] The child's despair is all-encompassing—because he does not know gradations, he feels either in darkest hell or gloriously happy—and therefore nothing but the most perfect everlasting bliss can combat his fear of total devastation at the moment.

[5.] One might rightly question [G. K.] Chesterton's belief in the innocence of children, but he is absolutely correct in observing that the appreciation of mercy for the unjust, while characteristic of a mature mind, baffles the child.[2]

I consider these generalizations both factually false and morally repugnant. How can something factually false also be morally repugnant? One way is for it to express an attitude of superiority that is morally inappropriate to one's dealings with other human beings. In my judgment, Betelheim's statements do that.

One day my students and I were discussing puzzles over infinity and how one might best respond to a child's questions about infinity. One student protested that this was a useless discussion, that before the age of twelve years or so, no child could possibly grasp the concept of infinity. To support her contention, she appealed to Bettelheim's assurance that young children "lack the abstract understanding required to make sense of [realistic explanations]." She recalled an episode from Bettelheim's book:

> In the fall of 1973, the comet Kohoutek was in the news. At that time a competent science teacher explained the

comet to a small group of highly intelligent second- and third-graders. Each child had carefully cut out a paper circle and had drawn on it the course of the planets around the sun; a paper ellipse, attached by a slit to the paper circle, represented the course of the comet. The children showed me the comet moving at an angle to the planets. When I asked them, the children told me that they were holding the comet in their hands, showing me the ellipse. When I asked how the comet which they were holding in their hands could also be in the sky, they were all nonplussed.

In their confusion, they turned to their teacher, who carefully explained to them that what they were holding in their hands, and had so diligently created, was only a model of the planets and the comet. The children all agreed that they understood this, and would have repeated it if questioned further. But whereas before they had regarded proudly this circle-cum-ellipse in their hands, they now lost all interest. Some crumpled the paper up, others dropped the model in the wastepaper basket. When the piece of paper had been the comet to them, they had all planned to take the model home to show their parents, but now it no longer had meaning for them.[3]

It is worth mentioning, by the way, that the concept of a model is an extremely interesting and rich subject for philosophical investigation. Many learned articles and books have been written on this topic and many more, I'm sure, will be written. The semantics of our talk of models and pictures is still only imperfectly understood. The topic has recently become more urgent because so much natural and social science is now conceived in terms of models: models of the atom, the human mind, the free-market economy, and so on.

Bettelheim gives no clue that he, or any other adult, might find anything interesting or problematic about the notion of a model: "When I asked how the comet which they were holding in their hands could also be in the sky, they were all nonplussed".

Imagine this bit of conversation: "The comet I now have in my hands is still in the sky; it's visible in the Southern Hemisphere. But the comet on the shelf over there burned up a century ago." That's an intelligible bit of conversation; but how can it be?

How *can* the comet I have in my hands also be in the sky? Asked in the derisive, dismissive way in which Bettelheim seems to have asked it, the question might shame any of us into crumpling up our models and dropping them into the wastebasket. Asked inquiringly, reflectively, or playfully, the question might introduce a fascinating field of inquiry, namely, the metaphysics and epistemology of models.

Incidentally, Thurber's *Many Moons* contains a delightful exchange between the Court Jester and the Princess Lenore. The Jester asks Lenore how the moon can be hanging from a chain around her neck and also be peeping through her window. The Princess replies with a series of poetic analogies that amuse, delight, and stimulate us to further reflection.

Back to my class and Bettelheim and to whether it is a waste of time to discuss the paradoxes of infinity with young children.

A few days later another student reported on Michael, the child from Chapter 3 who was worrying about whether the universe is infinite. What more effective response to Bettelheim's condescension could be imagined?

How can anyone who has spent so much of his working

life with children suppose them as limited in intellectual capacity as Bettelheim does? The best I can do by way of explanation is focus on the maxim "Ontogeny recapitulates phylogeny" (that is, the genesis or development of the individual recapitulates the stages in which the race has developed). Bettelheim, like Freud before him, seems to suppose this maxim true as a factual generalization about human development and also to find it compelling as a normative ideal. Indeed, he treats it both normatively and descriptively:

> What seems desirable for the individual is to repeat in his life span the process involved historically in the genesis of scientific thought. For a long time in his history man used emotional projections—such as gods—born of his immature hopes and anxieties to explain man, his society, and the universe; these explanations gave him a feeling of security. Then slowly, by his own social, scientific, and technological progress, man freed himself of the constant fear for his very existence. Feeling more secure in the world, and also within himself, man could now begin to question the validity of the images he had used in the past as explanatory tools. From there man's "childish" projections dissolved and more rational explanations took their place . . .
>
> Translated in terms of human behavior, the more secure a person feels within the world, the less he will need to hold on to "infantile" projections—mythical explanations or fairy-tale solutions to life's eternal problems—and the more he can afford to seek rational explanations.[4]

Philosophy, as we know it in our Western culture, began in the sixth century B.C. on the coast of Asia Minor, in what is now Turkey. It is fair to ask a recapitulationist like Bettelheim, "When in the development of a child is that child supposed to recapitulate the beginning of philosophy?" If the answer is "Not until puberty, when the child is first capable of abstract thinking," I have to say that, so far as I can tell, children of five, six, or, perhaps, seven years are much more likely to ask philosophical questions and make philosophical comments than children of twelve or fourteen years. The explanation for this phenomenon is complex.

In part, it has to do with the nature of philosophy. There is a certain innocence and naiveté about many, perhaps most, philosophical questions. This is something that adults, including college students, have to cultivate when they pick up their first book of philosophy. It is something natural to children.

Another part of the explanation has to do with the socialization processes in our society that turn children into adults. Adults discourage children from asking philosophical questions, first by being patronizing to them and then by directing their inquiring minds toward more "useful" investigations. Most adults aren't themselves interested in philosophical questions. They may be threatened by some of them. Moreover, it doesn't occur to most adults that there are questions that a child can ask that they can't provide a definitive answer to and that aren't answered in a standard dictionary or encyclopedia either.

So it is most implausible to think that children recapitulate the beginning of philosophy at puberty. Much earlier, then, say, at five or six years? A recapitulationist who supposes that a child recapitulates the beginning of philosophy at such an age ought to have much more respect for the minds of young children than Bettelheim does. I can only suppose that he is a recapitulationist who has omitted philosophy from the development of the race, and therefore from the development of the individual child.[5]

Bettelheim's view that young children are and ought to be preintellectual primitives reflects itself in the simple dichotomy with which he operates in *The Uses of Enchantment:* the dichotomy between fairy tales and realistic stories. I should emphasize that I share at least some of Bettelheim's enthusiasm for the psychological and existential richness of many fairy tales. I also share at least some of his disdain for the literary, psychological, and existential poverty of many so-called realistic stories. I am appalled, however, that anyone writing on children's literature could suppose that that domain is neatly divided into fairy stories crammed with psychological insights and goads to self-discovery and realistic stories that have no real meaning for a child's life. What about adventure stories? Detective stories? Ghost stories? Biographies? Poems? Tall tales? Histories?

The stories discussed in chapter 5 belong to the literature of fantasy, though they are not fairy stories. I have called their style "philosophical whimsy." Perhaps I could call them "intellectual adventure stories." What I have in mind is that they invite us to consider situations different from our everyday experience, even worlds unlike the familiar one about us—that is, to participate in what philosophers call "thought experiments" *(Gedankenexperimente).* Thought experiments are often a good way to trace conceptual connections and ruminate on philosophical puzzles. That is what these stories invite their readers to do.

A few more examples of intellectual adventure stories, presented in such a way as to emphasize their character as thought experiments or strings of thought experiments, might be helpful.

A VERY SIMPLE example of the kind of fantasy I have in mind is *Morris the Moose* by B. Wiseman. The story begins:

> One day Morris the Moose saw a cow . . .
> He said, "You're a funny-looking moose!"
> The cow said, "I'm a COW. I'm no MOOSE!"
> "You have four legs and a tail and things on your head. YOU'RE A MOOSE!"
> "But I say MOO!"
> Morris said, "I can say MOO too!"
> The cow said, "I give MILK to people. MOOSE DON'T DO THAT!!!"
> "So, YOU'RE A MOOSE WHO GIVES MILK TO PEOPLE!!"
> The cow said, "My MOTHER is a cow!"
> "She must be a MOOSE, because YOU'RE A MOOSE!"[6]

Morris and the cow meet a deer, who thinks that they are all deer. Then Morris, the cow, and the deer walk to a horse, who greets them with "Hello, you horses!"

The thought experiment in this story is simple yet profound. Suppose that someone called a moose a cow, or a horse a moose? What would be wrong with that? Anything?

Put rather grandly, the problem is the one of distinguishing between essential and accidental properties. An essential property of Morris is one that he can't lose without ceasing to exist and also, perhaps, one that he couldn't fail to have had. By contrast, an accidental property is one that he can lose without ceasing to exist and one that he might never have had.

Is "having things on your head" essential to a moose, say, Morris? If so, then the horse is definitely not a moose. But if "having things on your head" is only accidental, then Morris may be an antlered horse, or the horse a "bare-headed" moose.

The problem of essential and accidental properties is a problem in metaphysics. It can also be raised as a question of taxonomy, the classification of things. Is there a right way to classify things? If there is a single right way, how do we know what way that is? (This question brings us to epistemology.)

To be able to discuss biological taxonomy in any detail, one needs to know quite a lot about evolution and about variety in the biological world, including, among other things, what will mate with what. The principles of taxonomy and the philosophical issues they raise can also be discussed with nonbiological examples however.

Over dinner one evening, I put a question to my family:

What questions can you think of that are like these two?

Is a bicycle a tricycle without one of the wheels?

Is a snake a lizard without legs?

The responses came immediately:

Is a bicycle a motorbike without a motor?

Is a chair a rocker without runners?

Is a skirt a dress without a top?

Is lemonade a shandy without the beer?

Is horse-manure fertilizer without a purpose?

Is an ape a monkey without a tail?

Is a mouse a bat without wings?

Whimsical questions of this sort can introduce a

thoughtful discussion of the practical and philosophical problems of taxonomy. So can a delightful thought experiment like *Morris the Moose.*

AS A SECOND EXAMPLE of intellectual adventure I choose a little story called *How Big Is a Foot?* It's about a king who, unable to think of anything to get for his wife, the Queen ("who has everything"), invents the bed and has one made for her comfort. Asked how big it should be, the King makes the Queen lie down and, after stepping off her measurements, says, "Six feet by three feet." Unfortunately, the carpenter's feet are much smaller than the King's, so the bed, six carpenter's feet long and three carpenter's feet wide, is much too small for the Queen.[7]

The thought experiment this time is to imagine a world in which there are no standard measurements.

The notion of a paradigm—for example, a standard foot that, it seems, is necessarily a foot long, just as the standard yardstick in the Bureau of Standards in Washington, D.C., is, it seems, necessarily a yard long—has raised interesting philosophical issues ever since Plato. The idea of a paradigm foot (in the story a marble foot produced by "a famous sculptor") is one reason why *How Big Is a Foot?* is so philosophically interesting, but only one.

As I was reading the story recently to two six-year-olds, Abby and Heather, I came across this passage:

> When the Queen's birthday came near the King had a problem:
>> What could he give to Someone who had Everything?
>> The King thought and he thought and he thought.
>> Until suddenly, he had an idea!
> HE WOULD GIVE THE QUEEN A BED.

The queen did not have a bed because at the time beds had not been invented.

So even Someone who had Everything—did not have a bed.

I discussed with Abby and Heather the meaning of "invent." "It's to get an idea for making something nobody has ever made before," I told them.

Abby: You mean, there were no beds at all then?

Me: No beds at all.

H*eather:* But then the Queen didn't have everything if she didn't have a bed.

Abby (agreeing): No, she didn't have everything.

Abby (after musing and beginning to change her mind): Yeah, maybe she *did* have everything, if beds hadn't been invented.

Heather: No, she didn't have a bed, so she didn't have everything.

Abby: Well, maybe she had everything there *was*.

Does every unqualified occurrence of "everything" carry an implicit qualifier? Is it that the Queen, in having everything, had everything that existed at that time? Perhaps more plausibly, she had every *kind* of thing that she *wanted* that existed at *that time*. Russell once suggested that "the conception of the totality of things, or of the whole universe of entities and existents, is in some way illegitimate, and inherently contrary to logic."[8] If that is so, it may be well to suppose that "everything" is always at least implicitly qualified. Though the Queen didn't have a bed, she did have everything, that is, as Heather suggests, everything that there was (and, we might add, that she wanted).

AT THE BEGINNING of *Ozma of Oz,* another of Baum's intellectual adventure stories, Dorothy and her companion, a talking hen named "Billina," are shipwrecked on a strange island. There they soon come across an old tree:

> [It] was quite full of square paper boxes, which grew in clusters on all the limbs, and upon the biggest and ripest boxes the word "Lunch" could be read, in neat raised letters. This tree seemed to bear all the year around, for there were lunch-box blossoms on some of the branches, and on others tiny little lunch-boxes that were as yet quite green, and evidently not fit to eat until they had grown bigger.
>
> The leaves of this tree were all paper napkins, and it presented a very pleasing appearance to the hungry little girl.[9]

Dorothy picks a lunch box from the tree. In it she finds a ham sandwich, a piece of sponge cake, a pickle, a slice of new cheese, and an apple. A discussion follows about whether that particular box is fully ripe.

The inspiration for this thought experiment might have been a cry of exasperation, "And do you think lunches grow on trees?" In any case, the project is obvious: to imagine a world in which that most mundane of human products, the lunch box (complete with ham sandwich and the rest), is a product of nature. Baum invites us to consider what an organic process could and could not produce.

The theme of the book, one could say, is the difference between the natural and the artificial. This theme is pursued further when Dorothy and her friend encounter strange inhabitants of the island, who are called "wheelers." A wheeler is described in this way:

> It has the form of a man, except that it walked, or rather rolled, upon all fours, and its legs were the same length as its arms, giving them the appearance of the four legs

of a beast. Yet it was no beast that Dorothy had discovered, for the person was clothed most gorgeously in embroidered garments of many colors, and wore a straw hat perched jauntily upon the side of its head. But it differed from human beings in this respect, that instead of hands and feet there grew at the end of its arms and legs round wheels, and by means of these wheels it rolled very swiftly over the level ground. Afterward Dorothy found that these odd wheels were of the same hard substance that our finger-nails and toe-nails are composed of, and she also learned that creatures of this strange race were born in this queer fashion.[10]

The wheel is one of the most basic of human inventions. It does not imitate nature. Nowhere in nature is there a wheel. Why not? Baum is obviously intrigued by this fact, and he invites his readers to think about it, too.

Dorothy and her companion later encounter a wound-down mechanical man, whose label reads:

SMITH & TINKER'S

Patent Double-Action, Extra-Responsive, Thought-Creating, Perfect-Talking
MECHANICAL MAN

Fitted with our special Clock-Work Attachment.
Thinks, Speaks, Acts, and Does Everything but Live.[11]

Directions are given for using the mechanical man:

for THINKING: Wind the Clock-work Man under his left arm, (marked No. 1)

For SPEAKING: Wind the Clock-work Man under his right arm, (marked No. 2)

For WALKING and ACTION: Wind Clock-work in the middle of his back, (marked No. 3)[12]

Having blurred the line between organisms and artifacts to allow that trees might bear lunch boxes and four-legged creatures might grow wheels, Baum now imagines that something advertised as a nonliving artifact might function as human beings do when they think. This *Gedankenexperiment* is philosophically intriguing and instructive. It invites a consideration of whether a robot might be constructed that could think. If so, what would show that it thinks rather than merely simulates the behavior of thinking beings, including their verbal behavior? If not, why not? Baum all but asks these questions:

> "Which shall I wind up first?" she asked, looking again at the directions on the card.
>
> "Number One, I should think," returned Billina. "That makes him think, doesn't it?"
>
> "Yes," said Dorothy, and wound up Number One, under the left arm.
>
> "He doesn't seem any different," remarked the hen, critically.
>
> "Why, of course not; he is only thinking, now," said Dorothy.
>
> "I wonder what he is thinking about."
>
> "I'll wind up his talk, and then perhaps he can tell us," said the girl.
>
> So she wound up Number Two, and immediately the clock-work man said, without moving any part of his body except his lips:
>
> "Good morn-ing, lit-tle girl. Good morn-ing, Mrs. Hen."
>
> The words sounded a little hoarse and creakey, and they were uttered all in the same tone, without any change of expression whatever; but both Dorothy and Billina understood them perfectly.[13]

Baum's story is crammed with adventure, and much of it is intellectual. We are invited to explore a land of fantasy in a way that naturally brings us to a conceptual exploration of the real world about us. Could a lunch box, maybe even a lunch box with "lunch" printed on its side, be a product of nature? Would a pattern resembling the English word "lunch," if it were found to develop naturally on edible growths from a tree, mean "lunch"? And could a mechanical man that (who?) doesn't live, think? Baum asks that question and many more, some equally philosophical, by telling us a fantastical story.

BETTELHEIM, IN *The Uses of Enchantment,* provides an appropriate Freudian interpretation of every fairy tale that one has ever heard of, and many that one hasn't. As an exercise in Freudian literary criticism, Bettelheim's book is a virtuoso performance.

Perhaps Bettelheim could give *Ozma of Oz* a Freudian interpretation. But even if *Ozma of Oz* were interpreted psychoanalytically, its significance would not be exhausted. Nor would such an interpretation be sufficient to explain the seemingly permanent place of the Oz stories in children's literature. That the stories are wonderful tales of intellectual adventure counts, too.

Young children are indeed, as Bettelheim's work emphasizes, emotional beings. But they are more than that. They are, and have a right to be, thinking beings as well. A child whose literary diet includes tales of great emotional significance but no tales of intellectual adventure is disadvantaged and deprived in a way that Bettelheim has failed to appreciate.

7. Anxiety

SOME READERS may by now be intrigued with the idea of responding philosophically to a child's philosophical comment or question. But how does one do that? Doesn't one need philosophical training?

To do philosophy with a child, or with anyone else for that matter, is simply to reflect on a perplexity or a conceptual problem of a certain sort to see if one can remove the perplexity or solve the problem. Sometimes one succeeds, often one doesn't. Sometimes, getting clearer about one thing only makes it obvious that one is dreadfully unclear about something else.

Professional philosophers develop techniques for dealing with philosophical problems. Indeed, the use of special techniques can be very helpful. However, philosophers can become so preoccupied with their techniques that they lose sight of the questions and perplexities that first called the techniques forth. So skillfulness in using special techniques for dealing with philosophical questions may be an advantage, or it may get in the way.

Philosophers also study the writings of other philosophers to learn what they have to say about philosophical problems and perplexities. Ideally, a good grasp of the literature on a given question provides a rich context in which one can work out one's own answer or solution. But it doesn't always happen that way. At times, philosophers become so preoccupied with elucidating the views of others that they lose the original fascination they themselves once had with the problems. Again, they become so burdened with the weight of what their illustrious predecessors have had to say on a given topic that they lose confidence that they can find anything worth saying for themselves.

So, although there are certainly advantages to being a professional, what had promised to be an advantage can turn out to be or develop into a disadvantage. In any case, the amateur philosopher should feel no more embarrassment at doing philosophy than an amateur tennis player should feel about playing tennis. Above all, one shouldn't let the surmise that some great mind has already thought the thought that one is about to think spoil one's own excitement in coming up with it.

The equipment needed to do philosophy is basically the understanding that anyone with a moderately good command of the language and the concepts it expresses already has—plus great patience and a willingness to think about even the (apparently) simplest and most fundamental questions there are.

To do philosophy successfully with children requires that one rid oneself of all defensiveness. I am embarrassed if I cannot tell my child how to spell "tonsillectomy" or how to convert degrees Fahrenheit to degrees Celsius. But I should not be embarrassed to admit that I don't have ready an analysis of the concept of lying or a good, helpful response to the question "Where are dreams?" Instead, I should simply enlist the child's help so that we can try together to work out a satisfactory answer.

The combination of assets and liabilities that an adult brings to a philosophical encounter with a child makes for a very special relationship. The adult has a better command of the language than the child and, latently at least, a surer command of the concepts expressed in the language. It is the child, however, who has fresh eyes and ears for perplexity and incongruity. Children also have, typically, a degree of candor and spontaneity that is hard for the adult to match. Because each party has something important to contribute, the inquiry can easily become a genuinely joint venture, something otherwise quite rare in encounters between adults and children.

Some adults are not prepared to face a child stripped of the automatic presumption of adults' superiority in knowledge and experience. Others, however, may welcome a chance to pursue, if only for a few minutes, a question that, except for the child's expressed interest and curiosity in it, they would not have thought about at all.

Here I should inject a warning. I have been assuming that the comments and questions I have discussed are from children who are emotionally healthy and secure. The assumption may be unwarranted. Even a child who is usually confident and secure may have anxious moments and express these anxieties in a philosophical comment or question. The adult, whether parent or teacher or friend, should be alert to this possibility. Certainly, comments should not be responded to as if they had appeared in a vacuum. Sometimes assurances of loving concern should be included in the adult's response; and sometimes the adult should forget about the philosophy and concentrate on the child's emotional problems.

Often, however, the adult is justifiably confident that the child is quite capable of considering dispassionately the matter at hand. Even when one suspects that the comment or question carries considerable emotional freight, addressing the question, rather than treating it merely as an emotional symptom, may be part of showing proper respect for the child as a full-fledged human being.

This question, for example, is one that should be approached cautiously:

> JOHN (six years), reflecting on the fact that in addition to books, toys, and clothes he has two arms, two legs, and a head and that these are *his* toys, *his* arms, *his* head, and so on, asked, "Which part of me is really me?"

This question came shortly after the death of the family dog. John had probably been thinking about death, survival, and individual identity. He had realized, no doubt, that a person can lose an arm and a dog can lose a leg without either the person's ceasing to exist or the dog's ceasing to exist. John seemed to be interested, I judged from talking with him at the time, in whether there is any part of you that you can't lose without ceasing to exist.

Perhaps a child who raises a question like this is not secure enough at the moment to undertake a disinterested inquiry into the question of identity and survival. This does not mean that the question should be evaded or ignored. If the child is upset, evasion may only heighten the anxiety.

If one is the child's parent, one's religious beliefs may come into play at this point. If one has no religious beliefs or if one is not the child's parent, another kind of reassurance may be in order. It is well to remember, though, that what an adult intends to be reassurance may actually have the opposite effect. In many cases it is best to include an honest consideration of the question in whatever response seems appropriate.

In all of us there is, no doubt, an undercurrent of existential anguish. Sometimes our effort to protect children from thinking about death simply masks an effort to protect ourselves.[1]

John's question is richly suggestive. I shall pursue only two of the several lines of thinking that it suggests.

John is certainly distinct and separate from his toys, his books, even the clothes he has on. What is really John, one might say, is only (as a student of mine once wrote) what he takes with him into the bathtub.

Suppose, however, that John's toenails get clipped or his hair gets cut. When we throw away the toenail clippings or sweep up the hair cuttings, are we throwing away or sweeping up part of John? No, these bits are no longer part of John. They ceased being part of him when they were clipped or cut.

John's right arm is *his* arm and his head is *his* head. For something to be John's possession, doesn't John have to be distinct and separate from it? And if so, isn't he quite distinct and separate from his arms, his legs, his head—indeed, his body? Isn't he, in fact, the soul that owns this body? If so, then perhaps he can lose not only his toenail clippings and his hair cuttings but even his whole body.

Many people suppose this to be so. In fact, that it is so may be part of their religious faith. Perhaps it would be appropriate to witness to this faith to John.

It might also be worth noting, however, that merely being able to speak correctly of "my body" does not establish that I am something distinct from my body. A much more profound consideration would be required.

Consider this analogy. (In philosophy it is often helpful to consider analogies.) Suppose that we have a simple four-legged table. Here is *its* top, here are *its* four legs. What is "it"? There needn't be anything to the table other than its top and legs. In any case, that we can correctly speak of "its top" and "its legs" doesn't establish that the table is something separate and distinct from its top and its legs. (All this could, of course, become clear in a conversation with John.)

A so-called "possessive" pronoun ("its," "her," or "his") may, of course, express a relation of possession ("its food," "her toys," "his books"). But these pronouns may also be used to express the relation of whole to part ("its top," "her head," "his leg"). Likewise, the verb "to have" may be used to express the relation of possession ("John has a toy"). But it may also be used to express the relation of whole to part ("this table has a top"). Again, all this could come out in a conversation with John.

John's question—"Which part of me is really me?"—remains unanswered. What should one say?

I mentioned earlier that John seemed to have been thinking about what parts one can lose without ceasing to exist. This line of reflection could easily be turned into a consideration of piece-by-piece replacement. What part of a person or thing is such that if it were replaced, the original person or thing would cease to exist? What has already been said about the Tin Woodman and the ship of Theseus is, of course, directly relevant to this new question.

The table too is quite like the ship of Theseus, only much simpler. There seems to be no obvious point in the piece-by-piece replacement of its parts at which we would be forced to say that the old table ceases to exist.

What about John? Is there a point in the systematic replacement of organs and limbs at which we would be forced to say that the result of the next operation will be a new person? Most people, I suspect, would opt for the point at which the brain is replaced. This line of reasoning thus leads to saying that it is John's brain that is really John. On the basis of other conversations I have had with John, I think that he himself would have looked favorably on that result. For myself, I'm not so sure.

8. Naiveté

KATHERINE (almost four years) was given a helium-filled balloon at a fair. She carelessly let it go and was quite upset. After going to bed that night, she called her mother into her room and asked where the balloon was then: "What city is it over now? Is it in Vermont?" Mother: "I don't know where it is; it's probably not as far away as Vermont." Katherine: "Well, there aren't *three* skies, you know; there's only *one.*"

HOW MANY skies are there? The question is an odd one. Superficially, it's a bit like "How many oceans are there?" But, unlike that question, it can't be answered by looking in an atlas or an encyclopedia. It also seems somewhat like "How many moons are there?" But no book on meteorology or astronomy will tell us how many skies there are. The question is kooky.

United Airlines urges us to "fly the friendly skies of United" without telling us how many skies there are or even how many are covered by its route map.

We distinguish skies in various ways. We speak of the morning sky and the evening sky; we may say that the morning sky is overcast and the evening sky clear. A guide for stargazers might picture a summer sky and a winter sky, or perhaps a summer sky in northern latitudes at midnight, or just after dusk. Someone may say that Scottish skies are very different from Mediterranean skies.

What is the concept that finds expression in these sentences? Maybe it is primarily the notion of a visible hemisphere above the observer at a certain place and time and secondarily the visible contents of that hemisphere. When "sky" is understood to express the idea of a visible dome over some point on the earth's surface, we can say that there are many, many different skies, an infinitely large number of them, in fact.

There is also an inclination to say that the sky is the envelope of atmosphere that envelops the earth above building level. Anything that leaves *the* ground and goes up above buildings and trees goes up into *the* sky. When "sky" is used to express this notion, there is only one sky.

In a variation on the last idea, the sky is the clear air around the earth above building level. When "sky" is understood to express this idea, a break in the clouds may be said to enable us to see the sky.

Initially I said that the question "How many skies are there?" is kooky. Yet I have given it an answer of sorts. The sort of answer I've gone on to give it is a philosophical one—at least the beginning of a philosophical one. I've started a sketch of two or three concepts that "sky" could be said to express. Using one of these concepts, we could say with Katherine that there aren't three skies, there is only one. Using another, we would have to say there are an infinite number of skies.

Katherine's worry about the number of skies is discussed by Aristotle, who offers to prove that there is only one sky. He also says of *ouranos,* his word for the sky, or the heavens, that it has three senses (*On the Heavens* 278b10). Though some of what Aristotle discusses in *On the Heavens* is now the proper province of physics, chemistry, and astronomy, Katherine's concern is not.

Most people don't ask themselves or others how many skies there are. They learn early in life that this question, unlike "How many oceans are there?" is a kooky question.

Children like Katherine don't yet know that this is a deviant question. They stumble into philosophy from innocence rather than from the cultivation of naiveté that adults are limited to. They have not yet learned to reject as queer and misbegotten the many questions that philosophers have taught themselves to rescue from the wastebin of inquiry.

Let me try to bring this point about innocence and philosophy into line with one about innocence and poetry.

In chapter 1 of *The Child's Conception of the World* Piaget reports asking children between the ages of six and ten or eleven years whether words are strong.[1] He expects them to say, "Yes, some words are strong," at age six years or so and, "No, words are not strong," at age ten or eleven years. He expects them to answer so because he thinks that they begin by confusing a word with its meaning, a sign with the thing signified, and that only later do they learn to master and appreciate the important distinction. Thus, he believes that they will confuse the word "wind" with the wind and, noting that the wind is or may be strong, will conclude that the word "wind" is or may be strong. Piaget expects them to sort all this out gradually until they can say that although words themselves are not strong, some of the things that words name are strong.

Are words strong? Some are. An irate customer might complain to the manager of a store in strong words, even in very strong words. An English teacher might tell her pupils to favor Anglo-Saxon words over those of Latin origin on the grounds that the latter are weak, the former strong. And she would be right. Short words tend to be strong, long words weak.

"Strong" is itself a strong word, but not because it means strong. One of Piaget's young subjects, in fact, pointed out that the word "strong" is strong, but she seems not to have been given a chance to explain why she wanted to say that.

In addition to being a strong word, "strong" has an incredibly complex array of meanings and applications. Among the many things that may correctly be said to be strong are oxen, weight lifters, sunlight, colors, tea, arguments, convictions, customs, markets in certain commodities, irregular verbs, and ocean tides.

Adults naturally suppose that "strong" has one basic literal sense and a host of figurative senses and that the figurative ones can probably be accounted for by reference to the literal one. I suspect that Piaget did so. Perhaps a champion weight lifter is strong in the literal sense, whereas the words of an irate customer or stewed tea can be said to be strong only in a figurative sense.

In fact, the task of enumerating and sorting out all the senses of a rich and strong word like "strong" is extremely difficult. Saying just which uses are literal and which are figurative is also difficult. Showing in any helpful way how the allegedly figurative uses are related to the allegedly literal ones may not even be possible.

The literal-figurative distinction, of which perhaps nobody can give an entirely clear and coherent account, is one we learn to accept at an early age. Once we do accept it, we lose much of our natural curiosity about the wonderfully intricate ways in which the meanings of a word are related to each other.

A young child may find it striking that both a horse and a cup of tea may correctly be said to be strong. Given opportunity or encouragement, the child may write a poem that teases out and celebrates this curious fact. Or, given a different kind of stimulus or inclination, a child may wonder philosophically whether strong words are those that express strong feelings and whether strong feelings are those that move people to take strong actions. A child who assimilates from our culture the desensitizing thesis that many uses of words are merely figurative or metaphorical loses the fascination with the weft of words that inspires poetry and animates philosophy.

An adolescent or adult who writes poetry or does philosophy has to cultivate innocence to be able to puzzle and muse over the simplest ways we have of saying and seeing things. Cultivated innocence has many advantages over its natural counterpart. One is that it is not so easily thrown off balance by pretentious learning. But cultivated innocence is not the same as natural innocence. For at least this reason the poetry of children is different from the poetry of adults, and for at least this reason philosophy in children can't be exactly like philosophy in adults.

In arguing that philosophy is important to modern life and society, Robert Spaemann proposes that we conceive philosophy as "institutionalized naiveté."[2] To institutionalize naiveté is, presumably, to provide an institutional setting in which people will be encouraged to ask questions so basic that grappling with them seems to all of us some of the time, and to some of us all of the time, quite naive. Spaemann's suggestion is, I think, very helpful in several ways.

First, it brings out part of the reason why making room for philosophy in society is difficult. Philosophers seem to ask questions that no one wants to answer and to tell us what no one wants to know. Who needs them?

Second, it helps us to see what is important about making room for philosophy in a society. Sophistication may bring increased knowledge and, perhaps, a refined sensibility. But it may also encourage a cult of experts, dull sensitivity, and reward flatulence in thought and language. Every society needs a barefoot Socrates to ask childishly simple (and childishly difficult!) questions, to force its members to reexamine what they have been thoughtlessly taking for granted.

Spaemann's suggestion is appropriate in yet a third way. In children, naiveté comes naturally, without institutional encouragement. Therefore, with Spaemann's idea in mind, we might expect that philosophy too would come naturally to at least some children. It does.

9. Dialogues

MY HEAVY USE of short anecdotes in discussing philosophy and the young child may have created the very misleading impression that any attention children devote to philosophical questions is bound to be fitful and desultory. Certainly, the attention some children devote to philosophical matters is spasmodic. But there is impressive evidence of persistence and continuity in the thinking of others, as some of the fruits of relatively sustained reflection and inquiry in my son, John, demonstrate.

Over dinner one evening John, then nine years old, asked how we know what the French word *la table* means. (He had been learning French at school.)

"It means 'table,' " explained an older sister.

"But how do we know?" John persisted.

"For one thing, 'la table' looks like 'the table,' " suggested his sister.

"I know," returned John, "but they still might not have the same meaning. How do we know 'la table' means 'the table'?"

"Look it up in the dictionary!" was the reply.

John reflected a minute. "But how did the people who made up the dictionary find out what it means?"

John's sister, who was beginning her third foreign language, explained with an air of contrived patience that you learn when someone points to a table and says, "La table."

John wasn't satisfied. The context, however, was hardly suitable for philosophical inquiry. John's sister seemed, at that moment at least, uninterested in John's problem. In view of her decisive answers to John's queries, there seemed to be no good way to bring her to puzzlement without forcing her to lose face. I wanted to pursue the topic with John, but I waited until I had him alone.

When the two of us were alone over breakfast the next morning, John made clear that the move to give the meaning of "la table" by pointing to a table hadn't satisfied him because he thought that the pointing could be misunderstood.

"How do you know," John asked, "that it isn't the table *top* that the other guy is pointing to, or maybe the *color?*"

We talked a bit about what philosophers call "the ambiguity of ostension" (the ambiguity of giving the meaning of a word or phrase by pointing), and I promised John that I would take his bedtime reading from a little book on that subject.

For the next several nights John went to bed to readings from Augustine's *De magistro* (*Concerning the Teacher*), an engaging little dialogue between Augustine and his son, Adeodatus. Among the puzzles over language and meaning are several nice discussions of ambiguity in ostension. Toward the end of one of these, where the meaning of "birdcatching" is supposed to be demonstrated by a birdcatcher "doing his thing," Augustine says, in effect, that an observer who is intelligent enough will eventually catch on to what birdcatching is and hence what the word "birdcatching" means (10.32). John seemed to find that a good answer to his worries about ostension. If one is smart enough, he reasoned, one will eventually figure out what "la table" means.

Though we had certainly not, with this "insight," buried all reasonable worries about ostension, *De magistro* disappeared from the bedtime story hour, and there was no more talk about language or meaning for several months. Then one day I was driving home from the town center with John.

"The world's funny," he said, quite without warning.

"That's good," I replied. "You'll have a lot to amuse yourself over."

"No," said John, "I mean that lots of things in the world are funny to understand . . . like the road signs . . . SPEED LIMIT 30. . . . How do words mean what they mean?"

At first I couldn't figure out what it was about the meaning of road signs that John found perplexing. I developed several puzzles, one after the other. John would lay no claim to any of them.

"Take the word 'center,' " said John, finally. "What does it mean?"

"Well, I could give you another word for it," I said, "maybe 'middle.' "

"Yeah," said John, "but what does 'middle' mean?"

"Suppose I gave you a word for *it?*"

"Okay," said John, "but if all you can do is give more words, how do you know what any words mean?"

"Is this your problem?" I asked. "Suppose we came on the ruins of an old civilization. Suppose in the rubble we found something that looked like a dictionary—what looked like words all arranged neatly with what looked like definitions after them. One might learn that 'ablubaglub' means 'afister starterer' and that that means 'pinkerlaverstan' and so on. But even if you learned all those meanings so that if you were asked what so-and-so means you could reel off the right definition, you still wouldn't know what any—*any*—of the words meant. Is that your problem?"

Obviously, I had quite a bit invested in the attractiveness of this puzzle. But I didn't seem to have to apply any psychological pressure to get John to recognize it as his problem.

"Yeah, " said John, "just giving words for words doesn't really tell you what anything means."

I concluded from this discussion that we might well have another look at *De magistro*. Ostension, it seemed, had come to look problematic to John again. Otherwise, presumably, John would have been willing to say that we get from words to things by having the things that words name pointed out to us.

Instead of reading parts of *De magistro* again, though, I thought that we might try to rewrite parts of the dialogue so as to bring out John's worries in John's own language. We tried that for several evenings, again at bedtime. I would read some of *De magistro*, and then together we would try to make up a version to fit examples that John would supply. One example of something we wrote in that fashion follows:

John: What are words used for?
Daddy: For two purposes, I guess: to let somebody know something or else to learn something.

John: Okay, yeah, we do use words to let somebody know something. When I want to let you know I'm hungry, I say, "I'm hungry." (He thinks.) And when I say "Hi!" I'm letting you know something, too.

Daddy: Oh? What are you letting me know when you say "Hi!"?

John: I'm letting you know . . . uh, let me see . . . I'm letting you know I want to say "Hi!" (Ha-ha!) No, I'm letting you know I like you. Now, what else did you say words are used for?

Daddy: To learn something.

John: How do we do that?

Daddy: Well, what about when we ask a question? If I want to learn whether you are hungry, I can ask you, "Are you hungry?"

John: But aren't you just letting me know something again?

Daddy: What am I letting you know?

John: That you want to know whether I'm hungry.

Daddy: So you mean that what we use words for is always to let someone know something?

John: Yeah.

Daddy: What about singing? Don't we use words when we sing?

John: Yeah, sometimes anyway.

Daddy: Suppose you sing, "At McDonald's we do it all for you." What are you letting me know?

John: Uh . . . that at McDonald's they do it all for you.

Daddy: Suppose you sing, as you often do:

> Jingle bells,
> Batman smells,
> Robin laid an egg.
> Batmobile
> Lost its wheel
> And Joker got away.

What are you letting me know then?

John: A whole bunch of stupid stuff.

Daddy: Is what you are doing really letting me know that bells jingle or that Batman smells?

John: No, I'm making fun of Batman and Robin.

Daddy: And suppose you sing a song to yourself. Could you be letting *yourself* know something? Wouldn't you have to know already, and then there wouldn't be any point in telling yourself?

John: Maybe you're letting yourself know how well you can sing it.

Daddy: But can't you just be singing for fun without wanting to let yourself know anything?

John: Yeah, but then you're letting yourself know how you feel.

Here is the section of *De magistro* that we were imitating:

Augustine: What do you suppose is our purpose when we use words?

Adeodatus: The answer that occurs to me at the moment is, we want to let people know something, or we want to learn something.

Augustine: I agree at once with the former, for it is clear that when we use words we want to let somebody know something. But in what way do we show that we wish to learn?

Adeodatus: When we ask questions, of course.

Augustine: Even then, as I understand it, we want to let somebody know something. Do you ask a question for any other reason than to show the person questioned what you want to know?

Adeodatus: No.

Augustine: You see, then, that when we use words we desire nothing but to let someone know something.

Adeodatus: Not quite, perhaps. If speaking means using words, I see that we do so when we sing. Now we often sing when we are alone, with no one present to hear us; and then I cannot think we want to tell anyone anything.

Augustine: And yet I think there is a kind of teaching, and a most important kind, which consists in reminding people of something. I believe this will be made clear as our conversation proceeds. If, however, you do not think that we learn by remembering, or that he who reminds us of something really teaches us, I do not press the point. I assert that there are two reasons for our using words, either to teach, or to remind others or, it may be, ourselves. And we do this also when we sing. Don't you agree?

Adeodatus: Well, hardly. For I very rarely sing to remind myself of anything, almost always simply to give myself pleasure.[1]

I was dissatisfied with our parody. Although it does mimic Augustine, part of it is genuinely original. Yet it is hard to be clear about just what was included simply to imitate Augustine and what was included because John or I thought it interesting or appropriate. For example, John's final comment—"Yeah, but then [in singing] you're letting yourself know how you feel"—was original and very interesting.

So we abandoned the parody as a style of dialogue. Instead, we wrote several original dialogues that began with worries John had expressed and in which both of us tried our best to deal with those worries.

The procedure was this: First we would select one of John's questions for discussion. I would write it down. Then I would think of a response and write that down. Next I would read aloud the original question and my reply and ask John to think of a response. He would usually think for a little while and then come up with something, which I would write down.

John seemed to like this project. He cooperated cheerfully for several nights running. One morning over breakfast John's mother heard this exchange between John and his older sister:

John: Do you know what Daddy and I are doing?
Sister: What?
John: We're writing a dialogue.
Sister: About what?
John: About what we don't understand.

Our session produced several dialogues, two of which follow:

John: A long time ago, back in the days of cavemen, nobody could talk, right?
Daddy: You mean that nobody had a language?
John: Yeah. Well, how could anybody back then think?
Daddy: What about a small baby who hasn't yet learned to talk? What about *you* just before you learned to say your first word? Could you think?
John: No. Babies can't think when they're little.
Daddy: I suppose you don't know what the first word you learned was.
John: Yes I do—"appledoot" ["apple juice"].
Daddy: Okay, suppose that's right. Just before you first said "appledoot," do you suppose you could recognize the apple juice? What do you think?
John: Do you mean, so I think I would know that that was apple juice?
Daddy: Yes.
John: I suppose I would know that it's something my tummy would like, but I wouldn't be able to *think* that.
Daddy: Think of somebody in your quad at school whose name you don't know.
John: I know everybody's name in my quad.
Daddy: Well, think of somebody in Sunday School whose name you don't know.

John: Okay.

Daddy: How do you do that?

John: What do you mean?

Daddy: How do you think of that person whose name you don't know?

John: I have a picture of him in my mind.

Daddy: Do you think that you as a baby might have had a picture of apple juice [in mind]?

John reflects.

John: Let's go back to the guy I'm supposed to think of. I have to say to myself, "Think of a guy in Sunday School." I couldn't have done that if I didn't know any words.

Daddy: But couldn't a picture just come to you, without your saying anything to yourself.

John: You mean just appear? Bing?

Daddy: Yeah.

John: But it wouldn't mean anything. I couldn't say what it was or tell myself I was thinking of someone.

Daddy: I see what you mean. That's true, and very important. But suppose I am playing peekaboo with a baby. I hide behind a couch. The baby frowns. I appear suddenly and say, "Peekaboo!" The baby chuckles. I do it again. When I disappear, the baby frowns, and when I appear and say, "Peekaboo!" the baby chuckles. Isn't the baby thinking anything?

John: Did you really do that?

Daddy: Yes, I've often done that. I did that with you before you could talk. Don't you suppose you were thinking something like "There he is again" whenever I appeared and said "peekaboo!"?

John: Did you really do that?

Daddy: Yes, I often did it. Sometimes I would say, "Wher-er-ere's Daddy? Wher-er-ere's Daddy?" Then I would appear suddenly and say, "Peekaboo!"

John: Maybe a baby could understand *something* of what you are saying before he could say it himself.

Daddy: Do you mean he could say it to himself before he could say it out loud?

John: Yes . . . or some of it anyway.

After that session I decided to read to John the section of Augustine's *Confessions* that Wittgenstein quotes at the beginning of *Philosophical Investigations.*[2] I translated the rather stiff and pedantic prose of the English translation into words that I thought would sound more natural to John. Here is the stiff and pedantic prose:

> When they (my elders) named some object, and accordingly moved towards something, I saw this and I grasped that the thing was called by the sound they uttered when they meant to point it out. Their intention was shown by their bodily movements, as it were the natural language of all peoples: the expression of the face, the play of the eyes, the movement of other parts of the body, and the tone of voice which expresses our state of mind in seeking, having, rejecting, or avoiding something. Thus, as I heard words repeatedly used in their proper places in various sentences, I gradually learnt to understand what objects they signified; and after I had trained my mouth to form these signs, I used them to express my own desires. (1.8.13)

Together John and I then wrote a short dialogue:

John: He can't *know* that that's what he did. He figures out now that that is what he *probably* did. He doesn't *know* it.

Daddy: But isn't he right when he says he wanted something, for example, milk, before he knew the word for milk?

John: How could he want something? He'd have to think it to himself, and in words.

Daddy: When Arthur [our dog] sees me preparing his supper and comes up and wags his tail, don't you think he wants something to eat?

John: Yeah, but he has his own language.

Daddy: How do you know?

John: Because he wouldn't wag his tail if he didn't have a language.

Daddy: Do you mean that wagging his tail is a kind of sign language?

John: No, he has to tell himself to wag his tail. He has to have a language to do that.

When John came up with that last line, I thought immediately of a passage from Augustine's *De continentia:* "In fact we do many things with mouth closed, tongue at rest, voice in check; but we do nothing by action of the body that we have not said beforehand in the heart" (2.3).[3]

AS I WAS TYPING this chapter I decided to read parts of it to John. I asked him if he had thought about these matters recently. It had been a year and a half since we had written the dialogues together. John, at eleven years, had reached an age when it is much more unusual for children to raise philosophical questions or make philosophical comments.

"Not much," he said. He thought a bit and added, "I now believe babies can think, though."

"Oh," I said, "do you suppose they can talk to themselves before they can talk to us?"

"Yes," said John, "but they don't remember later how they did it. You don't remember what it was like to be a baby."

Apparently, philosophy persists, even though less obviously and less insistently than once. If John has trimmed his interests to conform to the expectations of the adult world around him, that's a shame. But if he has simply moved on to other interests, that's natural enough. There's more to life than philosophy.

Notes

1. Puzzlement

1. Augustine seems to have thought so; see his *Contra academicos* [Against the academicians] 3.11.26.

2. Bertrand Russell, *The Problems of Philosophy* (New York: Oxford University Press, 1959), p. 16.

3. Ludwig Wittgenstein, *Philosophical Investigations* (Oxford: Basil Blackwell, 1967), no. 123, p. 49.

4. Lewis Carroll, *Alice's Adventures in Wonderland & Through the Looking-Glass* (New York: New American Library, 1960), p. 23.

5. See Gareth Matthews, "A Medieval Theory of Vision," in *Studies in Perception,* ed. P. K. Machamer and R. G. Turnbull (Columbus: Ohio State University Press, 1978), pp. 186–199.

2. Play

1. A. A. Milne, *Winnie-the-Pooh* (London: Methuen, 1926), p. 32.

2. Susan Isaacs, *Intellectual Growth in Young Children* (London: Routledge & Kegan Paul, 1930), p. 355.

3. Ibid.

4. See G. E. L. Owen, "A Proof in the Peri Ideon," in *Studies in Plato's "Metaphysics,"* ed. R. E. Allen (London: Routledge & Kegan Paul, 1965), pp. 293–312.

5. Isaacs, *Intellectual Growth,* p. 151.

6. Ibid., p. 357.

7. Tom Stoppard, *Rosencrantz and Guildenstern Are Dead* (London: Faber & Faber, 1968), p. 78.

8. Isaacs, *Intellectual Growth,* p. 359.

9. Ibid., p. 360.

10. Ibid., p. 155.

3. Reasoning

1. Russell, *Problems of Philosophy,* pp. 22–23.

2. René Descartes, *Meditations on First Philosophy* (Indianapolis: Bobbs-Merrill, 1960), pp. 18, 19.

3. René Descartes, *Discourse on Method* (Indianapolis: Bobbs-Merrill, 1956), p. 21.

4. Carroll, *Alice's Adventures in Wonderland,* p. 165.

5. Norman Malcolm's reasoning in *Dreaming* (London: Routledge & Kegan Paul, 1959), seems somewhat like Tim's, though, of course, it is much more fully worked out: "When the sentence 'I am awake' is used to make a statement, there is not another possible statement which is its proper negation. There are not two things for me to decide between, one that I am awake the other that I am not awake. There is nothing to decide, no choice to make, nothing to find out" (p. 118). If there is "nothing to find out," there can be no real inquiry into whether one is dreaming. Malcolm's response to the dream problem thus seems to be a sophisticated cousin of Tim's.

6. Isaacs, *Intellectual Growth,* p. 355.

7. Another possible reconstruction would have Denis reasoning from

(a) Knowing is always right

and (6) to

(b) James is right (that is, isn't mistaken about whether P).

This reconstruction could rest on a weaker analysis of knowledge than is required for the one in the text. Sufficient for (a) is the idea that knowledge is true belief, whereas (4) requires infallibility.

8. In his dialogue "Theaetetus" Plato discusses three different analyses of knowledge: (*a*) knowledge is perception; (*b*) knowledge is true belief; and (*c*) knowledge is true belief with an account or justification, that is, knowledge is justified true belief.

9. Jean Piaget, *The Child's Conception of the World* (London: Routledge & Kegan Paul, 1951), p. 67.

10. Ibid., p. 66.

11. Bertrand Russell, "The Philosophy of Logical Atomism," in

Logic and Knowledge, ed. Robert C. Marsh (New York: G. P. Putnam's Sons, 1956), p. 243.

4. Piaget

1. Jean Piaget, *Play, Dreams, and Imitation in Childhood* (New York: W. W. Norton, 1951); *The Origins of Intelligence in Children* (New York: International Universities Press, 1952); *The Construction of Reality in the Child* (New York: Basic Books, 1954); *Child's Conception of the World.*

2. Ibid., p. 7.

3. Ibid., p. 10.

4. Ibid., pp. 37–38.

5. Ibid., pp. 38–39.

6. P. T. Geach, *Mental Acts* (London: Routledge & Kegan Paul, 1957); John B. Watson, *Behaviorism* (New York: W. W. Norton, 1970), chap. 10.

7. William James, *The Principles of Psychology* (New York: Dover Publications, 1950), vol. 1, chap. 9.

8. Piaget, *Child's Conception of the World,* pp. 38, 43–44.

9. Ibid., p. 27.

10. Ibid., pp. 166–167.

11. Ibid., pp. 167–168.

12. Ibid., pp. 110–111.

13. Ibid., p. 91.

5. Stories

1. There is certainly irony in my claim that Piaget is not sensitive to philosophical thinking in young children, as evidenced by the first two paragraphs of an early article, "Children's Philosophies," in *A Handbook of Child Psychology,* ed. Carl Murchison, 2nd ed. rev. (Worcester, Mass.: Clark University Press, 1933): "It goes without saying that the child does not actually work out any philosophy, properly speaking, since he never seeks to codify his reflections in anything like a system. Even as Tylor was wrong in speaking of the "savage philosophy" as that which concerns the mystic representations of primitive society, so also one cannot speak, other than by metaphor, of the philosophy of the child.

"And yet, however unconnected and incoherent the spontaneous remarks of children concerning the phenomena of nature, of the mind and of the origin of things, may be, we are able to discern in them some constant tendencies, reappearing with each new effort of reflection. These are the tendencies which we shall call 'children's philosophies' (p. 534)." The irony notwithstanding, I stick with my claim.

2. Frank Tashlin, *The Bear That Wasn't* (New York: Dover Publications, 1946), unpaginated.

3. John O. Nelson, "Can One Tell That He Is Awake by Pinching Himself?" *Philosophical Studies* 17 (1966):81–84. See also Michael Hodges and W. R. Carter, "Nelson on Dreaming a Pain," *Philosophical Studies* 20 (1969):43–46; and Jay Kantor, "Pinching and Dreaming," *Philosophical Studies* 21 (1970):28–32.

4. Montgomery Furth, "Elements of Eleatic Ontology," *Journal of the History of Philosophy* 6 (1968):111–132; see especially pp. 111–113.

5. L. Frank Baum, *The Wonderful Wizard of Oz* (New York: Dover Publications), 1960.

6. For a discussion of philosophical issues raised by the old story see Roderick M. Chisholm, "The Loose and Popular and the Strict and Philosophical Senses of Identity," in *Perception and Personal Identity*, ed. N. S. Care and R. H. Grimm (Cleveland: Case Western Reserve University Press, 1969), pp. 82–106.

7. John Locke, "Of Ideas of Identity and Diversity," *An Essay Concerning Human Understanding* (New York: Dover Publications, 1959), vol. 1, bk. 2, chap. 27, pp. 439–470.

8. James Thurber, *Many Moons* (New York: Harcourt Brace Jovanovich, 1971), unpaginated.

9. Isaacs, *Intellectual Growth*, pp. 360–361.

10. See John Austin's discussion of "The moon looks no bigger than a sixpence" in *Sense and Sensibilia* (Oxford: Oxford University Press, 1962), p. 41.

11. Milne, *Winnie-the-Pooh*, p. 91.

12. Carroll, *Alice's Adventures in Wonderland*, p. 186.

13. Wittgenstein, *Philosophical Investigations*, p. 18.

14. Arnold Lobel, *Frog and Toad Together* (New York: Harper & Row, 1972), pp. 30–41.

6. Fantasy

1. Bruno Bettelheim, *The Uses of Enchantment: The Meaning and Importance of Fairy Tales* (New York: Alfred A. Knopf, 1976).

2. Ibid., pp. 46, 47–48, 53, 126, 144.

3. Ibid., pp. 48–49.

4. Ibid., p. 51.

5. What one has to say about Piaget is much more complicated. Though he points out in his early "Children's Philosophies" and elsewhere parallels between the thinking of children and the thought of early philosophers, he says that "one cannot speak, other than by metaphor, of the philosophy of the child" (see chap. 5, n1). Moreover, as I tried to establish in chapter 4, Piaget, in *The Child's Conception of the World,* shows himself innocent of philosophical puzzlement and so, not surprisingly, innocent of genuine philosophical thinking in young children. Oddly, what Piaget says about adolescence suggests that genuine philosophy ought first to emerge at puberty. For example: "By comparison with a child, an adolescent is an individual who constructs systems and 'theories.' The child does not build systems. Those which he possesses are unconscious or preconscious in the sense that they are unformulable or unformulated so that only an external observer can understand them, while he himself never 'reflects' on them. In other words, he thinks concretely, he deals with each problem in isolation and does not integrate his solutions by means of any general theories from which he could abstract a common principle. By contrast, what is striking in the adolescent is his interest in theoretical problems not related to everyday realities . . . What is particularly surprising is his facility for elaborating abstract theories. Some write; they may create a philosophy, a political tract, a theory of aesthetics, or whatever. Others do not write; they talk . . . Up to this age (eleven–twelve), the operations of intelligence are solely 'concrete' . . . If a child at this level is asked to reason about simple hypotheses, presented verbally, he immediately loses ground and falls back on the prelogical intuition of the preschool child." ("The Mental Development of the Child," in *Six Psychological Studies,* ed. David Elkind [New York: Vintage Books, 1978], pp. 61–62). I find it hard to take these claims seriously. In defense, I can only offer the incidents I discuss in this book as evidence that Piaget's claims are unreasonable.

6. B. Wiseman, *Morris the Moose* (New York: Scholastic Book Services, 1973), unpaginated.

7. Rolf Myller, *How Big Is a Foot?* (Bloomfield, Conn.: Atheneum, 1962), unpaginated.

8. Bertrand Russell, *Principles of Mathematics* (New York: W. W. Norton, [1903]).

9. L. Frank Baum, *Ozma of Oz* (Chicago: Rand McNally, 1907), p. 27.

10. Ibid., p. 32.

11. Ibid., p. 43.

12. Ibid., p. 44.

13. Ibid., p. 46.

7. Anxiety

1. Sometimes the anxiety we think we find in children is a projection of our own anxiety. It is interesting to recall from chapter 1 Michael's response when he was asked about death.

8. Naiveté

1. Piaget, *Child's Conception of the World,* pp. 55–60.

2. Robert Spaemann, "Philosophie als institutionalisierte Naivitaet," *Philosophisches Jahrbuch* 81 (1974):139–142.

9. Dialogues

1. Augustine, *Augustine: Earlier Writings,* trans. J. H. S. Burleigh (Philadelphia: Westminster Press, 1953), p. 69.

2. Wittgenstein, *Philosophical Investigations,* p. 2.

3. See also Augustine *De trinitate* 9.7.12, 15.11.20.

Index